SIR GAWAYNE AND THE GREEN KNIGHT

IN THE ORIGINAL MIDDLE ENGLISH

Edited by

RICHARD MORRIS

CONTENTS

FYTTE THE FIRST

Siþen þe sege & þe assaut watȝ sesed at Troye,
Þe borȝ brittened & brent to brondeȝ & askeȝ,
Þe tulk þat þe trammes of tresoun þer wroȝt,

₄Watȝ tried for his tricherie, þe trewest on erthe;
Hit watȝ Ennias þe athel, & his highe kynde,
Þat siþen depreced prouinces, & patrounes bicome
Welneȝe of al þe wele in þe west iles,

₈Fro riche Romulus to Rome ricchis hym swyþe,
With gret bobbaunce þat burȝe he biges vpon fyrst,
& neuenes hit his aune nome, as hit now hat;
Ticius to Tuskan [turnes,] & teldes bigynnes;

₁₂Langaberde in Lumbardie lyftes vp homes;
& fer ouer þe French flod Felix Brutus
On mony bonkkes ful brode Bretayn he setteȝ,
wyth wynne;

1

₁₆Where werre, & wrake, & wonder,
Bi syþeʒ hatʒ wont þer-inne,
& oft boþe blysse & blunder
Ful skete hatʒ skyfted synne.

II.

₂₀Ande quen þis Bretayn watʒ bigged bi þis burn rych,
Bolde bredden þer-inne, baret þat lofden,
In mony turned tyme tene þat wroʒten;
Mo ferlyes on þis folde han fallen here oft

₂₄Þen in any oþer þat I wot, syn þat ilk tyme.
Bot of alle þat here bult of Bretaygne kynges
Ay watʒ Arthur þe hendest; as I haf herde telle;
For-þi an aunter in erde I attle to schawe,

₂₈Þat a selly in siʒt summe men hit holden,
& an outtrage awenture of Arthureʒ wondereʒ;
If ʒe wyl lysten þis laye bot on littel quile,
I schal telle hit, as-tit, as I in toun herde,

₃₂with tonge;
As hit is stad & stoken,
In stori stif & stronge,
With lel letteres loken,

₃₆In londe so hatʒ ben longe.

III.

Þis kyng lay at Camylot vpon kryst-masse,
With mony luflych lorde, ledeʒ of þe best,
Rekenly of þe rounde table alle þo rich breþer,

₄₀With rych reuel ory3t, & rechles merþes;
Þer tournayed tulkes bi-tyme3 ful mony,
Iusted ful Iolilé þise gentyle kni3tes,
Syþen kayred to þe court, caroles to make.

₄₄For þer þe fest wat3 ilyche ful fiften dayes,
With alle þe mete & þe mirþe þat men couþe a-vyse;
Such glaumande gle glorious to here,
Dere dyn vp-on day, daunsyng on ny3tes,

₄₈Al wat3 hap vpon he3e in halle3 & chambre3,
With lorde3 & ladies, as leuest him þo3t;
With all þe wele of þe worlde þay woned þer samen,
Þe most kyd kny3te3 vnder kryste seluen,

₅₂& þe louelokkest ladies þat euer lif haden,
& he þe comlokest kyng þat þe court haldes;
For al wat3 þis fayre folk in her first age,
on sille;

₅₆Þe hapnest vnder heuen,
Kyng hy3est mon of wylle,
Hit were now gret nye to neuen
So hardy a here on hille.

IV.

₆₀Wyle nw 3er wat3 so 3ep þat hit wat3 nwe cummen,
Þat day doubble on þe dece wat3 þe douth serued,
Fro þe kyng wat3 cummen with kny3tes in to þe halle,
Þe chauntre of þe chapel cheued to an ende;

₆₄Loude crye wat3 þer kest of clerke3 & oþer,
Nowel nayted o-newe, neuened ful ofte;
& syþen riche forth runnen to reche honde-selle,
3e3ed 3eres 3iftes on hi3, 3elde hem bi hond,

3

68Debated busyly aboute þo giftes;
Ladies laȝed ful loude, þoȝ þay lost haden,
& he þat wan watȝ not wrothe, þat may ȝe wel trawe.
Alle þis mirþe þay maden to þe mete tyme;

72When þay had waschen, worþyly þay wenten to sete,
Þe best burne ay abof, as hit best semed;
Whene Guenore ful gay, grayþed in þe myddes.
Dressed on þe dere des, dubbed al aboute,

76Smal sendal bisides, a selure hir ouer
Of tryed Tolouse, of Tars tapites in-noghe,
Þat were enbrawded & beten wyth þe best gemmes,
Þat myȝt be preued of prys wyth penyes to bye,

80in daye;
Þe comlokest to discrye,
Þer glent with yȝen gray,
A semloker þat euer he syȝe,

84Soth moȝt no mon say.

V.

Bot Arthure wolde not ete til al were serued,
He watȝ so Ioly of his Ioyfnes, & sum-quat child gered,
His lif liked hym lyȝt, he louied þe lasse

88Auþer to lenge lye, or to longe sitte,
So bi-sied him his ȝonge blod & his brayn wylde;
& also anoþer maner meued him eke,
Þat he þurȝ nobelay had nomen, ho wolde neuer ete

92Vpon such a dere day, er hym deuised were
Of sum auenturus þyng an vncouþe tale,
Of sum mayn meruayle, þat he myȝt trawe,

Of alderes, of armes, of oþer auenturus,

₉₆Oþer sum segg hym bi-soȝt of sum siker knyȝt,
To Ioyne wyth hym in iustyng in Iopardé to lay,
Lede lif for lyf, leue vchon oþer,
As fortune wolde fulsun hom þe fayrer to haue.

₁₀₀Þis watȝ [þe] kynges countenaunce where he in court were,
At vch farand fest among his fre meny,
in halle;
Þer-fore of face so fere.

₁₀₄He stiȝtleȝ stif in stalle,
Ful ȝep in þat nw ȝere,
Much mirthe he mas with alle.

VI.

Thus þer stondes in stale þe stif kyng his-seluen,

₁₀₈Talkkande bifore þe hyȝe table of trifles ful hende
There gode Gawan watȝ grayþed, Gwenore bisyde
& Agrauayn a la dure mayn on þat oþer syde sittes
Boþe þe kynges sister sunes, & ful siker kniȝtes;

₁₁₂Bischop Bawdewyn abof bi-gineȝ þe table,
& Ywan, Vryn son, ette wit hym-seluen;
Þise were diȝt on þe des, & derworþly serued,
& siþen mony siker segge at þe sidbordeȝ.

₁₁₆Þen þe first cors come with crakkyng of trumpes,
Wyth mony baner ful bryȝt, þat þer-bi henged,
Nwe nakryn noyse with þe noble pipes,
Wylde werbles & wyȝt wakned lote,

₁₂₀Þat mony hert ful hiȝe hef at her towches;

5

Dayntes dryuen þer-wyth of ful dere metes,
Foysoun of þe fresche, & on so fele disches,
Þat pine to fynde þe place þe peple bi-forne

124For to sette þe syluener, þat sere sewes halden,
on clothe;
Iche lede as he loued hym-selue
Þer laght with-outen loþe,

128Ay two had disches twelue,
Good ber, & bry3t wyn boþe.

VII.

Now wyl I of hor seruise say yow no more,
For veh wy3e may wel wit no wont þat þer were;

132An oþer noyse ful newe ne3ed biliue,
Þat þe lude my3t haf leue lif-lode to cach.
For vneþe wat3 þe noyce not a whyle sesed,
& þe fyrst cource in þe court kyndely serued,

136Þer hales in at þe halle dor an aghlich mayster,
On þe most on þe molde on mesure hyghe;
Fro þe swyre to þe swange so sware & so þik,
& his lyndes & his lymes so longe & so grete,

140Half etayn in erde I hope þat he were.
Bot mon most I algate mynn hym to bene,
& þat þe myriest in his muckel þat my3t ride;
For of bak & of brest al were his bodi sturne,

144Bot his wombe & his wast were worthily smale,
& alle his fetures fol3ande, in forme þat he hade,
ful clene;
For wonder of his hwe men hade,

6

₁₄₈Set in his semblaunt sene;
He ferde as freke were fade,
& ouer-al enker grene.

III.

Ande al grayþed in grene þis gome & his wedes,

₁₅₂A strayt cote ful streȝt, þat stek on his sides,
A mere mantile abof, mensked with-inne,
With pelure pured apert þe pane ful clene,
With blyþe blaunner ful bryȝt, & his hod boþe,

₁₅₆Þat watȝ laȝt fro his lokkeȝ, & layde on his schulderes
Heme wel haled, hose of þat same grene,
Þat spenet on his sparlyr, & clene spures vnder,
Of bryȝt golde, vpon silk bordes, barred ful ryche

₁₆₀& scholes vnder schankes, þere þe schalk rides;
& alle his vesture uerayly watȝ clene verdure,
Boþe þe barres of his belt & oþer blyþe stones,
Þat were richely rayled in his aray clene,

₁₆₄Aboutte hym-self & his sadel, vpon silk werkeȝ,
Þat were to tor for to telle of tryfles þe halue,
Þat were enbrauded abof, wyth bryddes & flyȝes,
With gay gaudi of grene, þe golde ay in myddes;

₁₆₈Þe pendauntes of his payttrure, þe proude cropure
His molaynes, & alle þe metail anamayld was þenne
Þe steropes þat he stod on, stayned of þe same,
& his arsounȝ al after, & his aþel sturtes,

₁₇₂Þat euer glemered & glent al of grene stones.
Þe fole þat he ferkkes on, fyn of þat ilke,
sertayn;

7

A grene hors gret & þikke,

₁₇₆A stede ful stif to strayne,
In brawden brydel quik,
To þe gome he watʒ ful gayn.

IX.

Wel gay watʒ þis gome gered in grene,

₁₈₀& þe here of his hed of his hors swete;
Fayre fannand fax vmbe-foldes his schulderes;
A much berd as a busk ouer his brest henges,
Þat wyth his hiʒlich here, þat of his hed reches,

₁₈₄Watʒ euesed al vmbe-torne, a-bof his elbowes,
Þat half his armes þer vnder were halched in þe wyse
Of a kyngeʒ capados, þat closes his swyre.
Þe mane of þat mayn hors much to hit lyke,

₁₈₈Wel cresped & cemmed wyth knottes ful mony,
Folden in wyth fildore aboute þe fayre grene,
Ay a herle of þe here, an oþer of golde;
Þe tayl & his toppyng twynnen of a sute,

₁₉₂& bounden boþe wyth a bande of a bryʒt grene,
Dubbed wyth ful dere stoneʒ, as þe dok lasted,
Syþen þrawen wyth a þwong a þwarle knot alofte,
Þer mony belleʒ ful bryʒt of brende golde rungen.

₁₉₆Such a fole vpon folde, ne freke þat hym rydes,
Watʒ neuer sene in þat sale wyth syʒt er þat tyme,
with yʒe;
He loked as layt so lyʒt,

₂₀₀So sayd al þat hym syʒe,

Hit semed as no mon my3t,
Vnder his dyntte3 dry3e.

X.

Wheþer hade he no helme ne hawb[e]rgh nauþer,

₂₀₄Ne no pysan, ne no plate þat pented to armes,
Ne no schafte, ne no schelde, to schwne ne to smyte,
Bot in his on honde he hade a holyn bobbe,
Þat is grattest in grene, when greue3 ar bare,

₂₀₈& an ax in his oþer, a hoge & vn-mete,
A spetos sparþe to expoun in spelle quo-so my3t;
Þe hede of an eln3erde þe large lenkþe hade,
Þe grayn al of grene stele & of golde hewen,

₂₁₂Þe bit burnyst bry3t, with a brod egge,
As wel schapen to schere as scharp rasores;
Þe stele of a stif staf þe sturne hit bi-grypte,
Þat wat3 wounden wyth yrn to þe wande3 ende,

₂₁₆& al bigrauen with grene, in gracios werkes;
A lace lapped aboute, þat louked at þe hede,
& so after þe halme halched ful ofte,
Wyth tryed tassele3 þerto tacched in-noghe,

₂₂₀On botoun3 of þe bry3t grene brayden ful ryche.
Þis haþel helde3 hym in, & þe halle entres,
Driuande to þe he3e dece, dut he no woþe,
Haylsed he neuer one, bot he3e he ouer loked.

₂₂₄Þe fyrst word þat he warp, "wher is," he sayd,
"Þe gouernour of þis gyng? gladly I wolde
Se þat segg in sy3t, & with hym self speke
raysoun."

228To kny3te3 he kest his y3e,
& reled hym vp & doun,
He stemmed & con studie,
Quo walt þer most renoun.

XI.

232Ther wat3 lokyng on lenþe, þe lude to be-holde,
For vch mon had meruayle quat hit mene my3t,
Þat a haþel & a horse my3t such a hwe lach,
As growe grene as þe gres & grener hit semed,

236Þen grene aumayl on golde lowande bry3ter;
Al studied þat þer stod, & stalked hym nerre,
Wyth al þe wonder of þe worlde, what he worch schulde.
For fele sellye3 had þay sen, bot such neuer are,

240For-þi for fantoum & fayry3e þe folk þere hit demed;
Þer-fore to answare wat3 ar3e mony aþel freke,
& al stouned at his steuen, & stonstil seten,
In a swoghe sylence þur3 þe sale riche

244As al were slypped vpon slepe so slaked hor lote3
in hy3e;
I deme hit not al for doute,
Bot sum for cortaysye,

248Bot let hym þat al schulde loute,
Cast vnto þat wy3e.

XII.

Þenn Arþour bifore þe hi3 dece þat auenture byholde3,
& rekenly hym reuerenced, for rad was he neuer,

10

₂₅₂& sayde, "wyȝe, welcum iwys to þis place,
Þe hede of þis ostel Arthour I hat,
Liȝt luflych adoun, & lenge, I þe praye,
& quat so þy wylle is, we schal wyt after."

₂₅₆"Nay, as help me," quod þe haþel, "he þat on hyȝe syttes,
To wone any quyle in þis won, hit watȝ not myn ernde;
Bot for þe los of þe lede is lyft vp so hyȝe,
& þy burȝ & þy burnes best ar holden,

₂₆₀Stifest vnder stel-gere on stedes to ryde,
Þe wyȝtest & þe worþyest of þe worldes kynde,
Preue for to play wyth in oþer pure laykeȝ;
& here is kydde cortaysye, as I haf herd carp,

₂₆₄& þat hatȝ wayned me hider, I-wyis, at þis tyme.
Ȝe may be seker bi þis braunch þat I bere here,
Þat I passe as in pes, & no plyȝt seche;
For had I founded in fere, in feȝtyng wyse,

₂₆₈I haue a hauberghe at home & a helme boþe,
A schelde, & a scharp spere, schinande bryȝt,
Ande oþer weppenes to welde, I wene wel als,
Bot for I wolde no were, my wedeȝ ar softer.

₂₇₂Bot if þou be so bold as alle burneȝ tellen,
Þou wyl grant me godly þe gomen þat I ask,
bi ryȝt."
Arthour con onsware,

₂₇₆& sayd, "sir cortays knyȝt,
If þou craue batayl bare,
Here fayleȝ þou not to fyȝt."

11

XIII.

"Nay, frayst I no fy3t, in fayth I þe telle,

₂₈₀Hit arn aboute on þis bench bot berdle3 chylder;
If I were hasped in armes on a he3e stede,
Here is no mon me to mach, for my3te3 so wayke.
For-þy I craue in þis court a crystmas gomen,

₂₈₄For hit is 3ol & nwe 3er, & here ar 3ep mony;
If any so hardy in þis hous holde3 hym-seluen,
Be so bolde in his blod, brayn in hys hede,
Þat dar stifly strike a strok for an oþer,

₂₈₈I schal gif hym of my gyft þys giserne ryche,
Þis ax, þat is heué in-nogh, to hondele as hym lykes,
& I schal bide þe fyrst bur, as bare as I sitte.
If any freke be so felle to fonde þat I telle,

₂₉₂Lepe ly3tly me to, & lach þis weppen,
I quit clayme hit for euer, kepe hit as his auen,
& I schal stonde hym a strok, stif on þis flet,
Elle3 þou wyl di3t me þe dom to dele hym an oþer,

₂₉₆barlay;
& 3et gif hym respite,
A twelmonyth & a day;—
Now hy3e, & let se tite

₃₀₀Dar any her-inne o3t say."

XIV.

If he hem stowned vpon fyrst, stiller were þanne
Alle þe hered-men in halle, þe hy3 & þe lo3e;

Þe renk on his rounce hym ruched in his sadel,

304& runisch-ly his rede yȝen he reled aboute,
Bende his bresed broȝeȝ, bly-cande grene,
Wayued his berde for to wayte quo-so wolde ryse.
When non wolde kepe hym with carp he coȝed ful hyȝe,

308Ande rimed hym ful richley, & ryȝt hym to speke:
"What, is þis Arþures hous," quod þe haþel þenne,
"Þat al þe rous rennes of, þurȝ ryalmes so mony?
Where is now your sourquydrye & your conquestes,

312Your gry[n]del-layk, & your greme, & your grete wordes?
Now is þe reuel & þe renoun of þe rounde table
Ouer-walt wyth a worde of on wyȝes speche;
For al dares for drede, with-oute dynt schewed!"

316Wyth þis he laȝes so loude, þat þe lorde greued;
Þe blod schot for scham in-to his schyre face
& lere;
He wex as wroth as wynde,

320So did alle þat þer were
Þe kyng as kene bi kynde,
Þen stod þat stif mon nere.

V.

Ande sayde, "haþel, by heuen þyn askyng is nys,

324& as þou foly hatȝ frayst, fynde þe be-houes;
I know no gome þat is gast of þy grete wordes.
Gif me now þy geserne, vpon godeȝ halue,
& I schal bayþen þy bone, þat þou boden habbes."

328Lyȝtly lepeȝ he hym to, & laȝt at his honde;

Þen feersly þat oþer freke vpon fote ly3tis.
Now hat3 Arthure his axe, & þe halme grype3,
& sturnely sture3 hit aboute, þat stryke wyth hit þo3t.

332Þe stif mon hym bifore stod vpon hy3t,
Herre þen ani in þe hous by þe hede & more;
Wyth sturne schere þer he stod, he stroked his berde,
& wyth a countenaunce dry3e he dro3 doun his cote,

336No more mate ne dismayd for hys mayn dinte3,
Þen any burne vpon bench hade bro3t hym to drynk
of wyne,
Gawan, þat sate bi þe quene,

334To þe kyng he can enclyne,
"I be-seche now with sa3e3 sene,
Þis melly mot be myne."

XVI.

"Wolde 3e, worþilych lorde," quod Gawan to þe kyng,

344"Bid me bo3e fro þis benche, & stonde by yow þere,
Þat I wyth-oute vylanye my3t voyde þis table,
& þat my legge lady lyked not ille,
I wolde com to your counseyl, bifore your cort ryche.

348For me þink hit not semly, as hit is soþ knawen,
Þer such an askyng is heuened so hy3e in your sale,
Þa33e 3our-self be talenttyf to take hit to your-seluen,
Whil mony so bolde yow aboute vpon bench sytten,

352Þat vnder heuen, I hope, non ha3er er of wylle,
Ne better bodyes on bent, þer baret is rered;
I am þe wakkest, I wot, and of wyt feblest,
& lest lur of my lyf, quo laytes þe soþe,

356Bot for as much as ȝe ar myn em, I am only to prayse,
No bounté bot your blod I in my bodé knowe;
& syþen þis note is so nys, þat noȝt hit yow falles,
& I haue frayned hit at yow fyrst, foldeȝ hit to me,

360& if I carp not comlyly, let alle þis cort rych,
bout blame."
Ryche to-geder con roun,
& syþen þay redden alle same,

364To ryd þe kyng wyth croun,
& gif Gawan þe game.

XVII.

Þen comaunded þe kyng þe knyȝt for to ryse;
& he ful radly vp ros, & ruchched hym fayre,

368Kneled doun bifore þe kyng, & cacheȝ þat weppen;
& he luflyly hit hym laft, & lyfte vp his honde,
& gef hym goddeȝ blessyng, & gladly hym biddes
Þat his hert & his honde schulde hardi be boþe.

372"Kepe þe cosyn," quod þe kyng, "þat þou on kyrf sette,
& if þou redeȝ hym ryȝt, redly I trowe,
Þat þou schal byden þe bur þat he schal bede after.
Gawan gotȝ to þe gome, with giserne in honde,

376& he baldly hym bydeȝ, he bayst neuer þe helder
Þen carppeȝ to sir Gawan þe knyȝt in þe grene,
"Refourme we oure for-wardes, er we fyrre passe.
Fyrst I eþe þe, haþel, how þat þou hattes,

380Þat þou me telle truly, as I tryst may?"
"In god fayth," quod þe goode knyȝt, "Gawan I hatte,
Þat bede þe þis buffet, quat-so bi-falleȝ after,

15

& at þis tyme twelmonyth take at þe anoþer,

384Wyth what weppen so þou wylt, & wyth no wyȝ elleȝ,
on lyue."
Þat oþer on-swareȝ agayn,
"Sir Gawan, so mot I þryue,

388As I am ferly fayn.
Þis dint þat þou schal dryue."

XVIII.

"Bigog," quod þe grene knyȝt, "sir Gawan, melykes,
Þat I schal fange at þy fust þat I haf frayst here;

392& þou hatȝ redily rehersed, bi resoun ful trwe,
Clanly al þe couenaunt þat I þe kynge asked,
Saf þat þou schal siker me, segge, bi þi trawþe,
Þat þou schal seche me þi-self, where-so þou hopes

396I may be funde vpon folde, & foch þe such wages
As þou deles me to day, bifore þis douþe ryche."
"Where schulde I wale þe," quod Gauan, "where is þy place?
I wot neuer where þou wonyes, bi hym þat me wroȝt,

400Ne I know not þe, knyȝt, þy cort, ne þi name.
Bot teche me truly þer-to, & telle me howe þou hattes,
& I schal ware alle my wyt to wynne me þeder,
& þat I swere þe for soþe, & by my seker traweþ."

404"Þat is in-nogh in nwe ȝer, hit nedes no more,"
Quod þe gome in þe grene to Gawan þe hende,
"ȝif I þe telle trwly, quen I þe tape haue,
& þou me smoþely hatȝ smyten, smartly I þe teche

408Of my hous, & my home, & myn owen nome,

16

Þen may þou frayst my fare, & forwardeȝ holde,
& if I spende no speche, þenne spedeȝ þou þe better,
For þou may leng in þy londe, & layt no fyrre,

412bot slokes;
Ta now þy grymme tole to þe,
& let se how þou cnokeȝ."
"Gladly sir, for soþe,"

416Quod Gawan; his ax he strokes.

XIX.

The grene knyȝt vpon grounde grayþely hym dresses,
A littel lut with þe hede, þe lere he discouereȝ,
His longe louelych lokkeȝ he layd ouer his croun.

420Let þe naked nec to þe note schewe.
Gauan gripped to his ax, & gederes hit on hyȝt,
Þe kay fot on þe folde he be-fore sette,
Let hit doun lyȝtly lyȝt on þe naked,

424Þat þe scharp of þe schalk schyndered þe bones,
& schrank þurȝ þe schyire grece, & scade hit in twynne,
Þat þe bit of þe broun stel bot on þe grounde.
Þe fayre hede fro þe halce hit [felle] to þe erþe,

428Þat fele hit foyned wyth her fete, þere hit forth roled;
Þe blod brayd fro þe body, þat blykked on þe grene;
& nawþer faltered ne fel þe freke neuer þe helder,
Bot styþly he start forth vpon styf schonkes,

432& ru[n]yschly he raȝt out, þere as renkkeȝ stoden,
Laȝt to his lufly hed, & lyft hit vp sone;
& syþen boȝeȝ to his blonk, þe brydel he cachcheȝ,
Steppeȝ in to stel bawe & strydeȝ alofte,

₄₃₆& his hede by þe here in his honde halde₃;
& as sadly þe segge hym in his sadel sette,
As non vnhap had hym ayled, þa₃ hedle₃ he we[re],
in stedde;

₄₄₀He brayde his bluk aboute,
Þat vgly bodi þat bledde,
Moni on of hym had doute,
Bi þat his resoun₃ were redde.

XX.

₄₄₄For þe hede in his honde he halde₃ vp euen,
To-ward þe derrest on þe dece he dresse₃ þe face,
& hit lyfte vp þe y₃e-lydde₃, & loked ful brode,
& meled þus much with his muthe, as ₃e may now here.

₄₄₈"Loke, Gawan, þou be grayþe to go as þou hette₃,
& layte as lelly til þou me, lude, fynde,
As þou hat₃ hette in þis halle, herande þise kny₃tes;
To þe grene chapel þou chose, I charge þe to fotte,

₄₅₂Such a dunt as þou hat₃ dalt disserued þou habbe₃,
To be ₃ederly ₃olden on nw ₃eres morn;
Þe kny₃t of þe grene chapel men knowen me mony;
For-þi me forto fynde if þou frayste₃, fayle₃ þou neuer,

₄₅₆Þer-fore com, oþer recreaunt be calde þe be-houeus."
With a runisch rout þe rayne₃ he torne₃,
Halled out at þe hal-dor, his hed in his hande,
Þat þe fyr of þe flynt fla₃e fro fole houes.

₄₆₀To quat kyth he be-com, knwe non þere,
Neuermore þen þay wyste fram queþen he wat₃ wonnen;
what þenne?
Þe kyng & Gawen þare,

₄₆₄At þat grene þay laȝe & grenne,
ȝet breued watȝ hit ful bare,
A meruayl among þo menne.

XI.

Þaȝ Arþer þe hende kyng at hert hade wonder,

₄₆₈He let no semblaunt be sene, bot sayde ful hyȝe
To þe comlych quene, wyth cortays speche,
"Dere dame, to day demay yow neuer;
Wel by-commes such craft vpon cristmasse,

₄₇₂Laykyng of enterludeȝ, to laȝe & to syng.
Among þise, kynde caroles of knyȝteȝ & ladyeȝ;
Neuer-þe-lece to my mete I may me wel dres,
For I haf sen a selly, I may not for-sake."

₄₇₆He glent vpon sir Gawen, & gaynly he sayde,
"Now sir, heng vp þyn ax, þat hatȝ in-nogh hewen."
& hit watȝ don abof þe dece, on doser to henge,
Þer alle men for meruayl myȝt on hit loke,

₄₈₀& bi trwe tytel þer-of to telle þe wonder.
Þenne þay boȝed to a borde þise burnes to-geder,
Þe kyng & þe gode knyȝt, & kene men hem serued
Of alle dayntyeȝ double, as derrest myȝt falle,

₄₈₄Wyth alle maner of mete & mynstralcie boþe;
Wyth wele walt þay þat day, til worþed an ende,
in londe.
Now þenk wel, sir Gawan,

₄₈₈For woþe þat þou ne wonde,
Þis auenture forto frayn,
Þat þou hatȝ tan on honde.

FYTTE THE SECOND

I.

This hanselle hat3 Arthur of auenturus on fyrst,

₄₉₂In 30nge 3er, for he 3erned 3elpyng to here,
Tha3 hym worde3 were wane, when þay to sete wenten;
Now ar þay stoken of sturne werk staf-ful her hond.
Gawan wat3 glad to be-gynne þose gomne3 in halle,

₄₉₆Bot þa3 þe ende be heuy, haf 3e no wonder;
For þa3 men ben mery in mynde, quen þay han mayn drynk,
A 3ere 3ernes ful 3erne, & 3elde3 neuer lyke,
Þe forme to þe fynisment folde3 ful selden.

₅₀₀For-þi þis 30l ouer-3ede, & þe 3ere after,
& vche sesoun serlepes sued after oþer;
After crysten-masse com þe crabbed lentoun,
Þat frayste3 flesch wyth þe fysche & fode more symple

₅₀₄Bot þenne þe weder of þe worlde wyth wynter hit þrepe3,

21

Colde clengeȝ adoun, cloudeȝ vp-lyften,
Schyre schedeȝ þe rayn in schowreȝ ful warme,
Falleȝ vpon fayre flat, flowreȝ þere schewen,

508Boþe groundeȝ & þe greueȝ grene ar her wedeȝ,
Bryddeȝ busken to bylde, & bremlych syngen,
For solace of þe softe somer þat sues þer after,
bi bonk;

512& blossumeȝ bolne to blowe,
Bi raweȝ rych & ronk,
Þen noteȝ noble in-noȝe,
Ar herde in wod so wlonk.

II.

516After þe sesoun of somer wyth þe soft wyndeȝ,
Quen ȝeferus syfleȝ hym-self on sedeȝ & erbeȝ,
Wela-wynne is þe wort þat woxes þer-oute.
When þe donkande dewe dropeȝ of þe leueȝ,

520To bide a blysful blusch of þe bryȝt sunne.
Bot þen hyȝes heruest, & hardenes hym sone.
Warneȝ hym for þe wynter to wax ful rype;
He dryues wyth droȝt þe dust for to ryse.

524Fro þe face of þe folde to flyȝe ful hyȝe;
Wroþe wynde of þe welkyn wrasteleȝ with þe sunne,
Þe leueȝ lancen fro þe lynde, & lyȝten on þe grounde,
& al grayes þe gres, þat grene watȝ ere;

528Þenne al rypeȝ & roteȝ þat ros vpon fyrst,
& þus ȝirneȝ þe ȝere in ȝisterdayeȝ mony,
& wynter wyndeȝ aȝayn, as þe worlde askeȝ
no sage.

22

532Til meȝel-mas mone,
Watȝ cumen wyth wynter wage;
Þen þenkkeȝ Gawan ful sone,
Of his anious uyage.

III.

536Ȝet quyl al-hal-day with Arþer he lenges,
& he made a fare on þat fest, for þe frekeȝ sake,
With much reuel & ryche of þe rounde table;
Knyȝteȝ ful cortays & comlych ladies,

540Al for luf of þat lede in longynge þay were,
Bot neuer-þe-lece ne þe later þay neuened bot merþe,
Mony ioyleȝ for þat ientyle iapeȝ þer maden.
For after mete, with mournyng he meleȝ to his eme,

544& spekeȝ of his passage, & pertly he sayde,
"Now, lege lorde of my lyf, leue I yow ask;
ȝe knowe þe cost of þis cace, kepe I no more
To telle yow teneȝ þer-of neuer bot trifel;

548Bot I am boun to þe bur barely to morne,
To sech þe gome of þe grene, as god wyl me wysse."
Þenne þe best of þe burȝ boȝed to-geder,
Aywan, & Errik, & oþer ful mony,

552Sir Doddinaual de Sauage, þe duk of Clarence,
Launcelot, & Lyonel, & Lucan þe gode,
Sir Boos, & sir Byduer, big men boþe,
& mony oþer menskful, with Mador de la Port.

556Alle þis compayny of court com þe kyng nerre,
For to counseyl þe knyȝt, with care at her hert;
Þere watȝ much derue doel driuen in þe sale,
Þat so worthe as Wawan schulde wende on þat ernde,

$_{560}$To dry3e a delful dynt, & dele no more
wyth bronde.
Þe kny3t mad ay god chere,
& sayde, "quat schuld I wonde,

$_{564}$Of destines derf & dere,
What may mon do bot fonde?"

IV.

He dowelle3 þer al þat day, and dresse3 on þe morn,
Aske3 erly hys arme3, & alle were þay bro3t

$_{568}$Fyrst a tule tapit, ty3t ouer þe flet,
& miche wat3 þe gyld gere þat glent þer alofte;
Þe stif mon steppe3 þeron, & þe stel hondole3,
Dubbed in a dublet of a dere tars,

$_{572}$& syþen a crafty capados, closed aloft,
Þat wyth a bry3t blaunner was bounden with-inne;
Þenne set þay þe sabatoun3 vpon þe segge fote3,
His lege3 lapped in stel with luflych greue3,

$_{576}$With polayne3 piched þer-to, policed ful clene,
Aboute his kne3 knaged wyth knote3 of golde;
Queme quyssewes þen, þat coyntlych closed
His thik þrawen þy3e3 with þwonges to-tachched;

$_{580}$& syþen þe brawden bryne of bry3t stel rynge3,
Vmbe-weued þat wy3, vpon wlonk stuffe;
& wel bornyst brace vpon his boþe armes,
With gode cowters & gay, & gloue3 of plate,

$_{584}$& alle þe godlych gere þat hym gayn schulde
Þat tyde;
Wyth ryche cote armure,

24

His gold sporeȝ spend with pryde,

588Gurde wyth a bront ful sure,
With silk sayn vmbe his syde.

When he watȝ hasped in armes, his harnays watȝ ryche,
Þe lest lachet ou[þ]er loupe lemed of golde;

592So harnayst as he watȝ he herkneȝ his masse,
Offred & honoured at þe heȝe auter;
Syþen he comeȝ to þe kyng & to his cort fereȝ,
Lacheȝ lufly his leue at lordeȝ & ladyeȝ;

596& þay hym kyst & conueyed, bikende hym to kryst.
Bi þat watȝ Gryngolet grayth, & gurde with a sadel,
Þat glemed ful gayly with mony golde frenges,
Ay quere naylet ful nwe for þat note ryched;

600Þe brydel barred aboute, with bryȝt golde bounden;
Þe apparayl of þe payttrure, & of þe proude skyrteȝ,
Þe cropore, & þe couertor, acorded wyth þe arsouneȝ;
& al watȝ rayled on red ryche golde nayleȝ,

604Þat al glytered & glent as glem of þe sunne.
Þenne hentes he þe holme, & hastily hit kysses,
Þat watȝ stapled stifly, & stoffed wyth-inne:
Hit watȝ hyȝe on his hede, hasped bihynde,

608Wyth a lyȝtli vrysoun ouer þe auentayle,
Enbrawden & bounden wyth þe best gemmeȝ,
On brode sylkyn borde, & bryddeȝ on semeȝ,
As papiayeȝ paynted pernyng bitwene,

612Tortors & trulofeȝ entayled so þyk,

25

As mony burde þer aboute had ben seuen wynter
in toune;
Þe cercle watȝ more o prys,

₆₁₆Þat vmbe-clypped hys croun,
Of diamaunteȝ a deuys,
Þat boþe were bryȝt & broun.

VI.

Then þay schewed hym þe schelde, þat was of schyr gouleȝ,

₆₂₀Wyth þe pentangel de-paynt of pure golde hweȝ;
He braydeȝ hit by þe baude-ryk, aboute þe hals kestes,
Þat bisemed þe segge semlyly fayre.
& quy þe pentangel apendeȝ to þat prynce noble,

₆₂₄I am in tent yow to telle, þof tary hyt me schulde;
Hit is a syngne þat Salamon set sum-quyle,
In bytoknyng of trawþe, bi tytle þat hit habbeȝ,
For hit is a figure þat haldeȝ fyue poynteȝ,

₆₂₈& vche lyne vmbe-lappeȝ & loukeȝ in oþer,
& ay quere hit is endeleȝ, & Englych hit callen
Ouer-al, as I here, þe endeles knot.
For-þy hit acordeȝ to þis knyȝt, & to his cler armeȝ,

₆₃₂For ay faythful in fyue & sere fyue syþeȝ,
Gawan watȝ for gode knawen, & as golde pured,
Voyded of vche vylany, wyth vertueȝ ennourned
in mote;

₆₃₆For-þy þe pen-tangel nwe
He ber in schelde & cote,
As tulk of tale most trwe,
& gentylest knyȝt of lote.

VII.

640Fyrst he watȝ funden fautleȝ in his fyue wytteȝ,
& efte fayled neuer þe freke in his fyue fyngres,
& alle his afyaunce vpon folde watȝ in þe fyue woundeȝ
Þat Cryst kaȝt on þe croys, as þe crede telleȝ;

644& quere-so-euer þys mon in melly watȝ stad,
His þro þoȝt watȝ in þat, þurȝ alle oþer þyngeȝ,
Þat alle his forsnes he fong at þe fyue ioyeȝ,
Þat þe hende heuen quene had of hir chylde;

648At þis cause þe knyȝt comlyche hade
In þe more half of his schelde hir ymage depaynted,
Þat quen he blusched þerto, his belde neuer payred.
Þe fyrst fyue þat I finde þat þe frek vsed,

652Watȝ fraunchyse, & felaȝschyp for-be al þyng;
His clannes & his cortaysye croked were neuer,
& pite, þat passeȝ alle poynteȝ, þyse pure fyue
Were harder happed on þat haþel þen on any oþer.

656Now alle þese fyue syþeȝ, forsoþe, were fetled on þis knyȝt,
& vchone halched in oþer, þat non ende hade,
& fyched vpon fyue poynteȝ, þat fayld neuer,
Ne samned neuer in no syde, ne sundred nouþ[er],

660With-outen ende at any noke [a]i quere fynde,
Where-euer þe gomen bygan, or glod to an ende.
Þer-fore on his schene schelde schapen watȝ þe knot,
Þus alle wyth red golde vpon rede gowleȝ,

664Þat is þe pure pentaungel wyth þe peple called,
with lore.
Now grayþed is Gawan gay,
& laȝt his launce ryȝt þore,

$_{668}$& gef hem alle goud day,
He wende for euer more.

VIII.

He sperred þe sted with þe spureȝ, & sprong on his way,
So stif þat þe ston fyr stroke out þer-after;

$_{672}$Al þat seȝ þat semly syked in hert,
& sayde soþly al same segges til oþer,
Carande for þat comly, "bi Kryst, hit is scaþe,
Þat þou, leude, schal be lost, þat art of lyf noble!

$_{676}$To fynde hys fere vpon folde, in fayth is not eþe;
Warloker to haf wroȝt had more wyt bene,
& haf dyȝt ȝonder dere a duk to haue worþed;
A lowande leder of ledeȝ in londe hym wel semeȝ,

$_{680}$& so had better haf ben þen britned to noȝt,
Hadet wyth an aluisch mon, for angardeȝ pryde.
Who knew euer any kyng such counsel to take,
As knyȝteȝ in cauelounȝ on cryst-masse gomneȝ!"

$_{684}$Wel much watȝ þe warme water þat waltered of yȝen,
When þat semly syre soȝt fro þo woneȝ
þat daye;
He made non abode,

$_{688}$Bot wyȝtly went hys way,
Mony wylsum way he rode,
Þe bok as I herde say.

IX.

Now rideȝ þis renk þurȝ þe ryalme of Logres,

692Sir Gauan on Godeʒ halue, þaʒ hym no gomen þoʒt;
Oft, leudleʒ alone, he lengeʒ on nyʒteʒ,
Þer he fonde noʒt hym byfore þe fare þat he lyked;
Hade he no fere bot his fole, bi frytheʒ & douneʒ,

696Ne no gome bot God, bi gate wyth to karp,
Til þat he neʒed ful noghe in to þe Norþe Waleʒ;
Alle þe iles of Anglesay on lyft half he haldeʒ,
& fareʒ ouer þe fordeʒ by þe for-londeʒ,

700Ouer at þe Holy-Hede, til he hade eft bonk
In þe wyldrenesse of Wyrale; wonde þer bot lyte
Þat auþer God oþer gome wyth goud hert louied.
& ay he frayned, as he ferde, at frekeʒ þat he met,

704If þay hade herde any karp of a knyʒt grene,
In any grounde þer-aboute, of þe grene chapel;
& al nykked hym wyth nay, þat neuer in her lyue
Þay seʒe neuer no segge þat watʒ of suche hweʒ

708of grene.
Þe knyʒt tok gates straunge,
In mony a bonk vnbene,
His cher ful oft con chaunge,

712Þat chapel er he myʒt sene.

X.

Mony klyf he ouer-clambe in contrayeʒ straunge,
Fer floten fro his frendeʒ fremedly he rydeʒ;
At vche warþe oþer water þer þe wyʒe passed,

716He fonde a foo hym byfore, bot ferly hit were,
& þat so foule & so felle, þat feʒt hym by-hode;
So mony meruayl hi mount þer þe mon fyndeʒ,

Hit were to tore for to telle of þe tenþe dole.

₇₂₀Sumwhyle wyth worme3 he werre3, & with wolues als,
Sumwhyle wyth wodwos, þat woned in þe knarre3,
Boþe wyth bulle3 & bere3, & bore3 oþer-quyle,
& etayne3, þat hym a-nelede, of þe he3e felle;

₇₂₄Nade he ben du3ty & dry3e, & dry3tyn had serued,
Douteles he hade ben ded, & dreped ful ofte.
For werre wrathed hym not so much, þat wynter was wors,
When þe colde cler water fro þe cloude3 schadden,

₇₂₈& fres er hit falle my3t to þe fale erþe;
Ner slayn wyth þe slete he sleped in his yrnes,
Mo ny3te3 þen in-noghe in naked rokke3,
Þer as claterande fro þe crest þe colde borne renne3,

₇₃₂& henged he3e ouer his hede in hard ÿsse-ikkles.
Þus in peryl, & payne, & plytes ful harde,
Bi contray carye3 þis kny3t, tyl kryst-masse euen,
al one;

₇₃₆Þe kny3t wel þat tyde,
To Mary made his mone.
Þat ho hym red to ryde,
& wysse hym to sum wone.

XI.

₇₄₀Bi a mounte on þe morne meryly he rydes,
Into a forest ful dep, þat ferly wat3 wylde,
Hi3e hille3 on vche a halue, & holt wode3 vnder,
Of hore oke3 fill hoge a hundreth to-geder;

₇₄₄Þe hasel & þe ha3-þorne were harled al samen,
With ro3e raged mosse rayled ay-where,

With mony brydde3 vnblyþe vpon bare twyges,
Þat pitosly þer piped for pyne of þe colde.

748Þe gome vpon Gryngolet glyde3 hem vnder,
Þur3 mony misy & myre, mon al hym one,
Carande for his costes, lest he ne keuer schulde,
To se þe seruy of þat syre, þat on þat self ny3t

752Of a burde wat3 borne, oure baret to quelle;
& þerfore sykyng he sayde, "I be-seche þe, lorde,
& Mary, þat is myldest moder so dere.
Of sum herber, þer he3ly I my3t here masse.

756Ande þy matyne3 to-morne, mekely I ask,
& þer-to prestly I pray my pater & aue,
& crede."
He rode in his prayere,

760& cryed for his mysdede,
He sayned hym in syþes sere,
& sayde "cros Kryst me spede!"

II.

Nade he sayned hym-self, segge, bot þrye,

764Er he wat3 war in þe wod of a won in a mote.
Abof a launde, on a lawe, loken vnder bo3e3,
Of mony borelych bole, aboute bi þe diches;
A castel þe comlokest þat euer kny3t a3te,

768Pyched on a prayere, a park al aboute,
With a pyked palays, pyned ful þik,
Þat vmbe-te3e mony tre mo þen two myle.
Þat holde on þat on syde þe haþel auysed,

772As hit schemered & schon þurȝ þe schyre okeȝ;
Þenne hatȝ he hendly of his helme, & heȝly he þonkeȝ
Iesus & say[nt] Gilyan, þat gentyle ar boþe,
Þat cortaysly hade hym kydde, & his cry herkened.

776"Now bone hostel," coþe þe burne, "I be-seche yow ȝette!"
Þenne gedereȝ he to Gryngolet with þe gilt heleȝ,
& he ful chauncely hatȝ chosen to þe chef gate,
Þat broȝt bremly þe burne to þe bryge ende,

780in haste;
Þe bryge watȝ breme vp-brayde,
Þe ȝateȝ wer stoken faste,
Þe walleȝ were wel arayed,

784Hit dut no wyndeȝ blaste.

XIII.

Þe burne bode on bonk, þat on blonk houed,
Of þe depe double dich þat drof to þe place,
Þe walle wod in þe water wonderly depe,

788Ande eft a ful huge heȝt hit haled vpon lofte,
Of harde hewen ston vp to þe tableȝ,
Enbaned vnder þe abataylment, in þe best lawe;
& syþen garyteȝ ful gaye gered bi-twene,

792Wyth mony luflych loupe, þat louked ful clene;
A better barbican þat burne blusched vpon neuer;
& innermore he be-helde þat halle ful hyȝe,
Towre telded bytwene trochet ful þik,

796Fayre fylyoleȝ þat fyȝed, & ferlyly long,
With coruon coprounes, craftyly sleȝe;
Chalk whyt chymnees þer ches he in-noȝe,

Vpon bastel roueȝ, þat blenked ful quyte;

800So mony pynakle payntet watȝ poudred ay quere,
Among þe castel carneleȝ, clambred so þik,
Þat pared out of papure purely hit semed.
Þe fre freke on þe fole hit fayr in-n[o]ghe þoȝt,

804If he myȝt keuer to com þe cloyster wyth-inne,
To herber in þat hostel, whyl halyday lested
auinant;
He calde, & sone þer com

808A porter pure plesaunt,
On þe wal his ernd he nome,
& haylsed þe knyȝt erraunt.

XIV.

"Gode sir," quod Gawan, "woldeȝ þou go myn ernde,

812To þe heȝ lorde of þis hous, herber to craue?"
"ȝe, Peter," quod þe porter, "& purely I trowe,
Þat ȝe be, wyȝe, welcum to won quyle yow lykeȝ."
Þen ȝede þat wyȝe aȝayn awyþe,

816& folke frely hym wyth, to fonge þe knyȝt;
Þay let doun þe grete draȝt, & derely out ȝeden,
& kneled doun on her knes vpon þe colde erþe,
To welcum þis ilk wyȝ, as worþy hom þoȝt;

820Þay ȝolden hym þe brode ȝate, ȝarked vp wyde,
& he hem raysed rekenly, & rod ouer þe brygge;
Sere seggeȝ hym sesed by sadel, quel he lyȝt,
& syþen stabeled his stede stif men in-noȝe.

824Knyȝteȝ & swyereȝ comen doun þenne,

33

For to bryng þis burne wyth blys in-to halle;
Quen he hef vp his helme, þer hi3ed in-noghe
For to hent hit at his honde, þe hende to seruen,

828His bronde & his blasoun boþe þay token.
Þen haylsed he ful hendly þo haþele3 vch one,
& mony proud mon þer presed, þat prynce to honour;
Alle hasped in his he3 wede to halle þay hym wonnen,

832Þer fayre fyre vpon flet fersly brenned.
Þenne þe lorde of þe lede loute3 fro his chambre,
For to mete wyth menske þe mon on þe flor;
He sayde, "3e ar welcum to welde as yow lyke3,

836Þat here is, al is yowre awen, to haue at yowre wylle
& welde."
"Graunt mercy," quod Gawayn,
"Þer Kryst hit yow for-3elde,"

840As freke3 þat semed fayn,
Ayþer oþer in arme3 con felde.

XV.

Gawayn gly3t on þe gome þat godly hym gret,
& þu3t hit a bolde burne þat þe bur3 a3te,

844A hoge haþel for þe none3, & of hyghe elde;
Brode bry3t wat3 his berde, & al beuer hwed,
Sturne stif on þe stryþþe on stal-worth schonke3,
Felle face as þe fyre, & fre of hys speche;

848& wel hym semed for soþe, as þe segge þu3t,
To lede a lortschyp in lee of leude3 ful gode.
Þe lorde hym charred to a chambre, & chefly cumaunde3
To delyuer hym a leude, hym lo3ly to serue;

852& þere were boun at his bode burneȝ in-noȝe,
Þat broȝt hym to a bryȝt boure, þer beddyng watȝ noble,
Of cortynes of clene sylk, wyth cler golde hemmeȝ,
& couertoreȝ ful curious, with comlych paneȝ,

856Of bryȝt blaunnier a-boue enbrawded bisydeȝ,
Rudeleȝ rennande on ropeȝ, red golde ryngeȝ,
Tapyteȝ tyȝt to þe woȝe, of tuly & tars,
& vnder fete, on þe flet, of folȝande sute.

860Þer he watȝ dispoyled, wyth specheȝ of myerþe,
Þe burn of his bruny, & of his bryȝt wedeȝ;
Ryche robes ful rad renkkeȝ hem broȝten,
For to charge, & to chaunge, & chose of þe best.

864Sone as he on hent, & happed þer-inne,
Þat sete on hym semly, wyth saylande skyrteȝ,
Þe ver by his uisage verayly hit semed
Wel neȝ to vche haþel alle on hwes,

868Lowande & lufly, alle his lymmeȝ vnder,
Þat a comloker knyȝt neuer Kryst made,
hem þoȝt;
Wheþen in worlde he were,

872Hit semed as he myȝt
Be prynce with-outen pere,
In felde þer felle men fyȝt.

XVI.

A cheyer by-fore þe chemné, þer charcole brenned,

876Watȝ grayþed for sir Gawan, grayþely with cloþeȝ,
Whyssynes vpon queldepoyntes, þa[t] koynt wer boþe;
& þenne a mere mantyle watȝ on þat mon cast,

Of a broun bleeaunt, enbrauded ful ryche,

₈₈₀& fayre furred wyth-inne with felleȝ of þe best,
Alle of ermyn in erde, his hode of þe same;
& he sete in þat settel semlych ryche,
& achaufed hym chefly, & þenne his cher mended.

₈₈₄Sone watȝ telded vp a tapit, on tresteȝ ful fayre,
Clad wyth a clene cloþe, þat cler quyt schewed,
Sanap, & salure, & syluer-in sponeȝ;
Þe wyȝe wesche at his wylle, & went to his mete

₈₈₈Seggeȝ hym serued semly in-noȝe,
Wyth sere sewes & sete, sesounde of þe best,
Double felde, as hit falleȝ, & fele kyn fischeȝ;
Summe baken in bred, summe brad on þe gledeȝ,

₈₉₂Summe soþen, summe in sewe, sauered with spyces,
& ay sawes so sleȝeȝ, þat þe segge lyked.
Þe freke calde hit a fest ful frely & ofte,
Ful hendely, quen alle þe haþeles re-hayted hym at oneȝ

₈₉₆as hende;
"Þis penaunce now ȝe take,
& eft hit schal amende;"
Þat mon much merþe con make.

₉₀₀For wyn in his hed þat wende.

XVII.

Þenne watȝ spyed & spured vpon spare wyse.
Bi preue poynteȝ of þat prynce, put to hym-seluen,
Þat he be-knew cortaysly of þe court þat he were,

₉₀₄Þat aþel Arthure þe hende haldeȝ hym one,

Þat is þe ryche ryal kyng of þe rounde table;
& hit watȝ Wawen hym-self þat in þat won sytteȝ,
Comen to þat krystmasse, as case hym þen lymped.

₉₀₈When þe lorde hade lerned þat he þe leude hade,
Loude laȝed he þerat, so lef hit hym þoȝt,
& alle þe men in þat mote maden much joye,
To apere in his presense prestly þat tyme,

₉₁₂Þat alle prys, & prowes, & pured þewes
Apendes to hys persoun, & praysed is euer,
By-fore alle men vpon molde, his mensk is þe most.
Vch segge ful softly sayde to his fere,

₉₁₆"Now schal we semlych se sleȝteȝ of þeweȝ,
& þe teccheles termes of talkyng noble,
Wich spede is in speche, vnspurd may we lerne,
Syn we haf fonged þat fyne fader of nurture;

₉₂₀God hatȝ geuen vus his grace godly for soþe,
Þat such a gest as Gawan graunteȝ vus to haue,
When burneȝ blyþe of his burþe schal sitte
& synge.

₉₂₄In menyng of manereȝ mere,
Þis burne now schal vus bryng,
I hope þat may hym here,
Schal lerne of luf-talkyng."

XVIII.

₉₂₈Bi þat þe diner watȝ done, & þe dere vp,
Hit watȝ neȝ at þe niyȝt neȝed þe tyme;
Chaplayneȝ to þe chapeles chosen þe gate,
Rungen ful rychely, ryȝt as þay schulden,

932To þe hersum euensong of þe hyȝe tyde.
Þe lorde loutes þerto, & þe lady als,
In-to a comly closet coyntly ho entreȝ;
Gawan glydeȝ ful gay, & gos þeder sone;

936Þe lorde laches hym by þe lappe, & ledeȝ hym to sytte,
& couþly hym knoweȝ, & calleȝ hym his nome,
& sayde he watȝ þe welcomest wyȝe of þe worlde;
& he hym þonkked þroly, & ayþer halched oþer.

940& seten soberly samen þe seruise-quyle;
Þenne lyst þe lady to loke on þe knyȝt.
Þenne com ho of hir closet, with mony cler burdeȝ,
Ho watȝ þe fayrest in felle, of flesche & of lyre,

944& of compas, & colour, & costes of alle oþer,
& wener þen Wenore, as þe wyȝe þoȝt.
He ches þurȝ þe chaunsel, to cheryche þat hende;
An oþer lady hir lad bi þe lyft honde,

948Þat watȝ alder þen ho, an auncian hit semed,
& heȝly honowred with haþeleȝ aboute.
Bot yn-lyke on to loke þo ladyes were,
For if þe ȝonge watȝ ȝep, ȝolȝe watȝ þat oþer;

952Riche red on þat on rayled ay quere,
Rugh ronkled chekeȝ þat oþer on rolled;
Kerchofes of þat on wyth mony cler perleȝ
Hir brest & hir bryȝt þrote bare displayed,

956Schon schyrer þen snawe, þat scheder on hilleȝ;
Þat oþer wyth a gorger watȝ gered ouer þe swyre,
Chymbled ouer hir blake chyn with mylk-quyte vayles,
Hir frount folden in sylk, enfoubled ay quere,

960Toret & treieted with tryfleȝ aboute,

Þat noȝt watȝ bare of þat burde bot þe blake broȝes.
Þe tweyne yȝen, & þe nase, þe naked lyppeȝ,
& þose were soure to se, & sellyly blered;

964A mensk lady on molde mon may hir calle,
for gode;
Hir body watȝ schort & þik.
Hir buttokeȝ bay & brode,

968More lykker-wys on to lyk,
Watȝ þat scho hade on lode.

XIX.

When Gawayn glyȝt on þat gay, þat graciously loked,
Wyth leue laȝt of þe lorde he went hem aȝaynes;

972Þe alder he haylses, heldande ful lowe,
Þe loueloker he lappeȝ a lyttel in armeȝ,
He kysses hir comlyly, & knyȝtly he meleȝ;
Þay kallen hym of a quoyntaunce, & he hit quyk askeȝ

976To be her seruaunt sothly, if hem-self lyked.
Þay tan hym bytwene hem, wyth talkyng hym leden
To chambre, to chemné, & chefly þay asken
Spyceȝ, þat vn-sparely men speded hom to bryng,

980& þe wynne-lych wyne þer-with vche tyme.
Þe lorde luflych aloft lepeȝ ful ofte,
Mynned merthe to be made vpon mony syþeȝ.
Hent heȝly of his hode, & on a spere henged,

984& wayned hom to wynne þe worchip þer-of,
Þat most myrþe myȝt mene þat crystenmas whyle;
"& i schal fonde, bi my fayth, to fylter wyth þe best,
Er me wont þe wedeȝ, with help of my frendeȝ."

988Þus wyth laȝande loteȝ þe lorde hit tayt makeȝ,
For to glade sir Gawayn with gomneȝ in halle
þat nyȝt;
Til þat hit watȝ tyme,

992Þe kyng comaundet lyȝt,
Sir Gawen his leue con nyme,
& to his bed hym diȝt.

XX.

On þe morne, as vch mon myneȝ þat tyme,

996[Þ]at dryȝtyn for oure destyné to deȝe watȝ borne,
Wele waxeȝ in vche a won in worlde, for his sake;
So did hit þere on þat day, þurȝ dayntes mony;
Boþe at mes & at mele, messes ful quaynt

1000Derf men vpon dece drest of þe best.
Þe olde auncian wyf heȝest ho sytteȝ;
Þe lorde lufly her by lent, as I trowe;
Gawan & þe gay burde to-geder þay seten,

1004Euen in-myddeȝ, as þe messe metely come;
& syþen þurȝ al þe sale, as hem best semed,
Bi vche grome at his degre grayþely watȝ serued.
Þer watȝ mete, þer watȝ myrþe, þer watȝ much ioye,

1008Þat for to telle þerof hit me tene were,
& to poynte hit ȝet I pyned me parauenture;
Bot ȝet I wot þat Wawen & þe wale burde
Such comfort of her compaynye caȝten to-geder,

1012Þurȝ her dere dalyaunce of her derne wordeȝ,
Wyth clene cortays carp, closed fro fylþe;
& hor play watȝ passande vche prynce gomen,

in vayres;

₁₀₁₆Trumpeȝ & nakerys,
Much pypyng þer repayres,
Vche mon tented hys,
& þay two tented þayres.

XXI.

₁₀₂₀Much dut watȝ þer dryuen þat day & þat oþer,
& þe þryd as þro þronge in þerafter;
Þe ioye of sayn Ioneȝ day watȝ gentyle to here,
& watȝ þe last of þe layk, leudeȝ þer þoȝten.

₁₀₂₄Þer wer gestes to go vpon þe gray morne,
For-þy wonderly þay woke, & þe wyn dronken,
Daunsed ful dreȝly wyth dere caroleȝ;
At þe last, when hit watȝ late, þay lachen her leue,

₁₀₂₈Vchon to wende on his way, þat watȝ wyȝe stronge.
Gawan gef hym god-day, þe god mon hym lachcheȝ,
Ledes hym to his awen chambre, þ[e] chymné bysyde,
& þere he draȝeȝ hym on-dryȝe, & derely hym þonkkeȝ,

₁₀₃₂Of þe wynne worschip & he hym wayned hade,
As to honour his hous on þat hyȝe tyde,
& enbelyse his burȝ with his bele chere.
"I-wysse sir, quyl I leue, me worþeȝ þe better,

₁₀₃₆Þat Gawayn hatȝ ben my gest, at Goddeȝ awen fest."
"Grant merci sir," quod Gawayn, "in god fayth hit is yowreȝ,
Al þe honour is your awen, þe heȝe kyng yow ȝelde;
& I am wyȝe at your wylle, to worch youre hest,

₁₀₄₀As I am halden þer-to, in hyȝe & in loȝe,
bi riȝt."

41

Þe lorde fast can hym payne,
To holde lenger þe kny3t,

1044To hym answre3 Gawayn,
Bi non way þat he my3t.

XXII.

Then frayned þe freke ful fayre at him-seluen,
Quat derne dede had hym dryuen, at þat dere tyme,

1048So kenly fro þe kynge3 kourt to kayre al his one,
Er þe halidaye3 holly were halet out of toun?
"For soþe sir," quod þe segge, "3e sayn bot þe trawþe
A he3e ernde & a hasty me hade fro þo wone3,

1052For I am sumned my selfe to sech to a place,
I wot in worlde wheder warde to wende, hit to fynde;
I nolde, bot if I hit negh my3t on nw3eres morne,
For alle þe londe in-wyth Logres, so me oure lorde help!

1056For-þy, sir, þis enquest I require yow here,
Þat 3e me telle with trawþe, if euer 3e tale herde
Of þe grene chapel, quere hit on grounde stonde3,
& of þe kny3t þat hit kepes, of colour of grene?

1060Þer wat3 stabled bi statut a steuen vus by-twene,
To mete þat mon at þat mere, 3if I my3t last;
& of þat ilk nw3ere hot neked now wonte3,
& I wolde loke on þat lede, if God me let wolde,

1064Gladloker, bi Godde3 sun, þen any god welde!
For-þi, I-wysse, bi 30wre wylle, wende me bi-houes,
Naf I now to busy bot bare þre daye3,
& me als fayn to falle feye as fayly of myyn ernde."

₁₀₆₈Þenne laȝande quod þe lorde, "now leng þe by-houes,
For I schal teche yow to þa[t] terme bi þe tymeȝ ende,
Þe grene chapayle vpon grounde, greue yow no more;
Bot ȝe schal be in yowre bed, burne, at þyn ese,

₁₀₇₂Quyle forth dayej, & ferk on pe fyrst of pe ȝere,
& cum to þat merk at mydmorn, to make quat yow likeȝ
in spenne;
Dowelleȝ whyle new ȝeres daye,

₁₀₇₆& rys, & raykeȝ þenne,
Mon schal yow sette in waye,
Hit is not two myle henne."

XIII.

Þenne watȝ Gawan ful glad, & gomenly he laȝed,—

₁₀₈₀"Now I þonk yow þryuandely þurȝ alle oþer þynge,
Now acheued is my chaunce, I schal at your wylle
Dowelle, & elleȝ do quat ȝe demen."
Þenne sesed hym þe syre, & set hym bysyde,

₁₀₈₄Let þe ladieȝ be fette, to lyke hem þe better;
Þer watȝ seme solace by hem-self stille;
Þe lorde let for luf loteȝ so myry,
As wyȝ þat wolde of his wyte, ne wyst quat he myȝt.

₁₀₈₈Þenne he carped to þe knyȝt, criande loude,
"ȝe han demed to do þe dede þat I bidde;
Wyl ȝe halde þis hes here at þys oneȝ?"
"ȝe sir, for-soþe," sayd þe segge trwe,

₁₀₉₂"Whyl I byde in yowre borȝe, be bayn to ȝow[r]e hest."
"For ȝe haf trauayled," quod þe tulk, "towen fro ferre,
& syþen waked me wyth, ȝe arn not wel waryst,

43

Nauþer of sostnaunce ne of slepe, soþly I knowe;

1096 ȝe schal lenge in your lofte, & lyȝe in your ese,
To morn quyle þe messe-quyle, & to mete wende,
When ȝe wyl, wyth my wyf, þat wyth yow schal sitte,
& comfort yow with compayny, til I to cort torne,

1100 ȝe lende;
& I schal erly ryse,
On huntyng wyl I wende."
Gauayn granteȝ alle þyse,

1104 Hym heldande, as þe hende.

XXIV.

"ȝet firre," quod þe freke, "a forwarde we make;
Quat-so-euer I wynne in þe wod, hit worþeȝ to youreȝ,
& quat chek so ȝe acheue, chaunge me þer-forne;

1108 Swete, swap we so, sware with trawþe,
Queþer, leude, so lymp lere oþer better."
"Bi God," quod Gawayn þe gode, "I grant þer-tylle,
& þat yow lyst forto layke, lef hit me þynkes.

1112 "Who bringeȝ vus þis beuerage, þis bargayn is maked:"
So sayde þe lorde of þat lede; þay laȝed vchone,
Þay dronken, & daylyeden, & dalten vntyȝtel,
Þise lordeȝ & ladyeȝ, quyle þat hem lyked;

1116 & syþen with frenkysch fare & fele fayre loteȝ
Þay stoden, & stemed, & stylly speken,
Kysten ful comlyly, & kaȝten her leue.
With mony leude ful lyȝt, & lemande torches,

1120 Vche burne to his bed watȝ broȝt at þe laste,

44

ful softe;
To bed ȝet er þay ȝede,
Recorded couenaunteȝ ofte;

1124Þe olde lorde of þat leude,
Cowþe wel halde layk a-lofte.

FYTTE THE THIRD

I.

Ful erly bifore þe day þe folk vp-rysen,
Gestes þat go wolde, hor grome3 þay calden,

1128& þay busken vp bilyue, blonkke3 to sadel,
Tyffen he[r] takles, trussen her males,
Richen hem þe rychest, to ryde alle arayde,
Lepen vp ly3tly, lachen her brydeles,
Each goes where it pleases him best.

1132Vche wy3e on his way, þer hym wel lyked.
Þe leue lorde of þe londe wat3 not þe last,
A-rayed for þe rydyng, with renkke3 ful mony;
Ete a sop hastyly, when he hade herde masse,

1136With bugle to bent felde he buske3 by-lyue;
By þat þat any day-ly3t lemed vpon erþe,
He with his haþeles on hy3e horsses weren.
Þenne þise cacheres þat couþe, cowpled hor hounde3,

1140Vnclosed þe kenel dore, & calde hem þer-oute,
Blwe bygly in bugleȝ þre bare mote;
Braches bayed þerfore, & breme noyse maked,
& þay chastysed, & charred, on chasyng þat went;

1144A hundreth of hunteres, as I haf herde telle,
of þe best;
To trystors vewters ȝod,
Couples huntes of kest,

1148Þer ros for blasteȝ gode,
Gret rurd in þat forest.

II.

At þe fyrst quethe of þe quest quaked þe wylde;
Der drof in þe dale, doted for drede,

1152Hiȝed to þe hyȝe, bot heterly þay were
Restayed with þe stablye, þat stoutly ascryed;
Þay let þe hertteȝ haf þe gate, with þe hyȝe hedes,
Þe breme bukkeȝ also, with hor brode paumeȝ;

1156For þe fre lorde hade de-fende in fermysoun tyme,
Þat þer schulde no mon mene to þe male dere.
Þe hindeȝ were halden in, with hay & war,
Þe does dryuen with gret dyn to þe depe sladeȝ;

1160Þer myȝt mon se, as þay slypte, slentyng of arwes,
At vche [þat] wende vnder wande wapped a flone,
Þat bigly bote on þe broun, with ful brode hedeȝ,
What! þay brayen, & bleden, bi bonkkeȝ þay deȝen.

1164& ay rachches in a res radly hem folȝes,
Huntereȝ wyth hyȝe horne hasted hem after,
Wyth such a crakkande kry, as klyffes haden brusten;

48

What wylde so at-waped wy3es þat schotten,

₁₁₆₈Wat3 al to-raced & rent, at þe resayt.
Bi þay were tened at þe hy3e, & taysed to þe wattre3,
Þe lede3 were so lerned at þe lo3e trysteres,
& þe gre-hounde3 so grete, þat geten hem bylyue,

₁₁₇₂& hem to fylched, as fast as freke3 my3t loke,
þer ry3t.
Þe lorde for blys abloy
Ful oft con launce & ly3t,

₁₁₇₆& drof þat day wyth Ioy
Thus to þe derk ny3t.

II.

Þus layke3 þis lorde by lynde wode3 eue3,
& G. þe god mon, in gay bed lyge3,

₁₁₈₀Lurkke3 quyl þe day-ly3t lemed on þe wowes,
Vnder couertour ful clere, cortyned aboute;
& as in slomeryng he slode, sle3ly he herde
A littel dyn at his dor, & derfly vpon;

₁₁₈₄& he heue3 vp his hed out of þe cloþes,
A corner of þe cortyn he ca3t vp a lyttel,
& wayte3 warly þider-warde, quat hit be my3t.
Hit wat3 þe ladi, loflyest to be-holde,

₁₁₈₈Þat dro3 þe dor after hir ful dernly[1] & stylle,
& bo3ed to-warde þe bed; & þe burne schamed.
& layde hym doun lystyly, & let as he slepte.
& ho stepped stilly. & stel to his bedde,

₁₁₉₂Kest vp þe cortyn, & creped with-inne,

& set hir ful softly on þe bed-syde,
& lenged þere selly longe, to loke quen he wakened.
Þe lede lay lurked a ful longe quyle,

1196Compast in his concience to quat þat cace my3t
Mene oþer amount, to meruayle hym þo3t;
Bot 3et he sayde in hym-self, "more semly hit were
To aspye wyth my spelle [in] space quat ho wolde."

1200þen he wakenede, & wroth, & to hir warde torned,
& vn-louked his y3e-lydde3, & let as hym wondered,
& sayned hym, as bi his sa3e þe sauer to worthe,
with hande;

1204Wyth chynne & cheke ful swete,
Boþe quit & red in-blande,
Ful lufly con ho lete,
Wyth lyppe3 smal la3ande.

IV.

1208"God moroun, sir Gawayn," sayde þat fayr lady,
"3e ar a sleper vn-sly3e, þat mon may slyde hider;
Now ar 3e tan astyt, bot true vus may schape,
I schal bynde yow in your bedde, þat be 3e trayst:"

1212Al la3ande þe lady lanced þo bourde3.
"Goud moroun g[aye]," quod Gawayn þe blyþe,
"Me schal worþe at your wille, & þat me wel lyke3,
For I 3elde me 3ederly, & 3e3e after grace,

1216& þat is þe best, be my dome, for me by-houe3 nede;"
& þus he bourded a-3ayn with mony a blyþe la3ter.
"Bot wolde 3e, lady louely, þen leue me grante,
& de-prece your prysoun, & pray hym to ryse,

50

₁₂₂₀I wolde boȝe of þis bed, & busk me better,
I schulde keuer þe more comfort to karp yow wyth."
"Nay, for soþe, beau sir," sayd þat swete,
"ȝe schal not rise of your bedde, I rych yow better,

₁₂₂₄I schal happe yow here þat oþer half als,
& syþen karp wyth my knyȝt þat I kaȝt haue;
For I wene wel, Iwysse, sir Wawen ȝe are,
Þat alle þe worlde worchipeȝ, quere-so ȝe ride;

₁₂₂₈Your honour, your hendelayk is hendely praysed
With lordeȝ, wyth ladyes, with alle þat lyf bere.
& now ȝe ar here, iwysse, & we bot oure one;
"My lorde & his ledeȝ ar on lenþe faren,

₁₂₃₂Oþer burneȝ in her bedde, & my burdeȝ als,
Þe dor drawen, & dit with a derf haspe;
& syþen I haue in þis hous hym þat al lykeȝ,
I schal ware my whyle wel, quyl hit lasteȝ,

₁₂₃₆with tale;
ȝe ar welcum to my cors,
Yowre awen won to wale,
Me be-houeȝ of fyne force,

₁₂₄₀Your seruaunt be & schale."

V.

"In god fayth," quod Gawayn, "gayn hit me þynkkeȝ,
Þaȝ I be not now he þat ȝe of speken;
To reche to such reuerence as ȝe reherce here

₁₂₄₄I am wyȝe vn-worþy, I wot wel my-seluen;
Bi God, I were glad, & yow god þoȝt,
At saȝe oþer at seruyce þat I sette myȝt

To þe plesaunce of your prys, hit were a pure ioye."

1248"In god fayth, sir Gawayn," quod þe gay lady,
"Þe prys & þe prowes þat pleseʒ al oþer,
If I hit lakked, oþer set at lyʒt, hit were littel daynté;
Bot hit ar ladyes in-noʒe, þat leuer wer nowþe

1252Haf þe hende in hor holde, as I þe habbe here,
To daly witt derely your daynté wordeʒ,
Keuer hem comfort, & colen her careʒ,
Þen much of þe garysourn oþer golde þat þay hauen;

1256Bot I louue þat ilk lorde þat þe lyfte haldeʒ,
I haf hit holly in my honde þat al desyres,
þurʒe grace."
Scho made hym so gret chere,

1260Þat watʒ so fayr of face,
Þe knyʒt with speches skere,
A[n]swared to vche a cace.

VI.

"Madame," quod þe myry mon, "Mary yow ʒelde,

1264For I haf founden, in god fayth, yowre fraunchis nobele,
& oþer ful much of oþer folk fongen hor dedeʒ;
Bot þe daynté þat þay delen for my disert nysen,
Hit is þe worchyp of your-self, þat noʒt bot wel conneʒ."

1268"Bi Mary," quod þe menskful, "me þynk hit anoþer;
For were I worth al þe wone of wymmen alyue,
& al þe wele of þe worlde were in my honde,
& I schulde chepen & chose, to cheue me a lorde,

1272For þe costes þat I haf knowen vpun þe knyʒt here,

Of bewté, & debonerté, & blyþe semblaunt,
& þat I haf er herkkened, & halde hit here trwee,
Þer schulde no freke vpon folde bifore yow be chosen."

₁₂₇₆"I-wysse, worþy," quod þe wyȝe, "ȝe haf waled wel better,
Bot I am proude of þe prys þat ȝe put on me,
& soberly your seruaunt my souerayn I holde yow,
& yowre knyȝt I be-com, & Kryst yow for-ȝelde."

₁₂₈₀Þus þay meled of much-quat, til myd-morn paste,
& ay þe lady let lyk, a hym loued mych;
Þe freke ferde with defence, & feted ful fayre.
Þaȝ I were burde bryȝtest, þe burde in mynde hade,

₁₂₈₄Þe lasse luf in his lode, for lur þat he soȝt,
boute hone;
Þe dunte þat schulde hym deue,
& nedeȝ hit most be done;

₁₂₈₈Þe lady þenn spek of leue.
He granted hir ful sone.

VII.

Þenne ho gef hym god-day, & wyth a glent laȝed.
& as ho stod, ho stonyed hym wyth ful stor wordeȝ:

₁₂₉₂"Now he þat spedeȝ vche spech, þis disport ȝelde yow!
Bot þat ȝe be Gawan, hit gotȝ in mynde."
"Quer-fore?" quod þe freke, & freschly he askeȝ,
Ferde lest he hade fayled in fourme of his castes;

₁₂₉₆Bot þe burde hym blessed, & bi þis skyl sayde,
"So god as Gawayn gaynly is halden,
& cortaysye is closed so clene in hym-seluen,
Couth not lyȝtly haf lenged so long wyth a lady,

₁₃₀₀Bot he had craued a cosse, bi his courtaysye,
Bi sum towch of summe tryfle, at sum tale3 ende."
Þen quod Wowen, "I-wysse, worþe as yow lyke3,
I schal kysse at your comaundement, as a kny3t falle3,

₁₃₀₄& fire lest he displese yow, so plede hit no more."
Ho comes nerre with þat, & cache3 hym in arme3,
Loute3 luflych adoun, & þe leude kysse3;
Þay comly bykennen to Kryst ayþer oþer;

₁₃₀₈Ho dos hir forth at þe dore, with-outen dyn more.
& he ryches hym to ryse, & rapes hym sone,
Clepes to his chamberlayn, choses his wede,
Bo3e3 forth, quen he wat3 boun, blyþely to masse,

₁₃₁₂& þenne he meued to his mete, þat menskly hym keped,
& made myry al day til þe mone rysed,
with game;
With neuer freke fayrer fonge,

₁₃₁₆Bitwene two so dyngne dame,
Þe alder & þe 3onge,
Much solace set þay same.

VIII.

And ay þe lorde of þe londe is lent on his gamne3,

₁₃₂₀To hunt in holte3 & heþe, at hynde3 barayne,
Such a sowme he þer slowe bi þat þe sunne heldet,
Of dos & of oþer dere, to deme were wonder.
Þenne fersly þay flokked in folk at þe laste,

₁₃₂₄& quykly of þe quelled dere a querré þay maked;
Þe best bo3ed þerto, with burne3 in-noghe,
Gedered þe grattest of gres þat þer were,

& didden hem derely vndo, as þe dede aske3;

1328Serched hem at þe asay, summe þat þer were,
Two fyngeres þay fonde of þe fowlest of alle;
Syþen þay slyt þe slot, sesed þe erber,
Schaued wyth a scharp knyf, & þe schyre knitten;

1332Syþen rytte þay þe foure lymmes, & rent of þe hyde,
Þen brek þay þe bale, þe bale3 out token,
Lystily forlancyng, & bere of þe knot;
Þay gryped to þe gargulun, & grayþely departed

1336Þe wesaunt fro þe wynt-hole, & walt out þe gutte3;
Þen scher þay out þe schuldere3 with her scharp knyue3,
Haled hem by a lyttel hole, to haue hole sydes;
Siþen britned þay þe brest, & brayden hit in twynne,

1340& eft at þe gargulun bigyne3 on þenne,
Ryue3 hit vp radly, ry3t to þe by3t,
Voyde3 out þe a-vanters, & verayly þerafter
Alle þe ryme3 by þe rybbe3 radly þay lance;

1344So ryde þay of by resoun bi þe rygge bone3,
Euenden to þe haunche, þat henged alle samen,
& heuen hit vp al hole, & hwen hit of þere,
& þat þayneme for þe noumbles, bi nome as I trowe,

1348bi kynde;
Bi þe by3t al of þe þy3es,
Þe lappe3 þay lance bi-hynde,
To hewe hit in two þay hy3es,

1352Bi þe bak-bon to vnbynde.

IX.

Boþe þe hede & þe hals þay hwen of þenne,
& syþen sunder þay þe sydeȝ swyft fro þe chyne,
& þe corbeles fee þay kest in a greue;

1356Þenn þurled þay ayþer þik side þurȝ, bi þe rybbe,
& henged þenne a[y]þer bi hoȝes of þe fourcheȝ,
Vche freke for his fee, as falleȝ forto haue.
Vpon a felle of þe fayre best, fede þay þayr houndes,

1360Wyth þe lyuer & þe lyȝteȝ, þe leþer of þe pauncheȝ,
& bred baþed in blod, blende þer amongeȝ;
Baldely þay blw prys, bayed þayr rachcheȝ,
Syþen fonge þay her flesche folden to home,

1364Strakande ful stoutly mony stif moteȝ.
Bi þat þe daylyȝt watȝ done, þe douthe watȝ al wonen
In-to þe comly castel, þer þe knyȝt bideȝ
ful stille;

1368Wyth blys & bryȝt fyr bette,
Þe lord is comen þer-tylle,
When Gawayn wyth hym mette,
Þer watȝ bot wele at wylle.

X.

1372Thenne comaunded þe lorde in þat sale to samen alle þe
meny,
Boþe þe ladyes on loghe to lyȝt with her burdes,
Bi-fore alle þe folk on þe flette, frekeȝ he beddeȝ
Verayly his venysoun to fech hym byforne;

1376& al godly in gomen Gaway[n] he called,

56

Teche3 hym to þe tayles of ful tayt bestes,
Schewe3 hym þe schyree grece schorne vpon rybbes.
"How paye3 yow þis play? haf I prys wonnen?

1380Haue I þryuandely þonk þur3 my craft serued?"
"3e I-wysse," quod þat oþer wy3e, "here is wayth fayrest
Þat I se3 þis seuen 3ere in sesoun of wynter."
"& al I gif yow, Gawayn," quod þe gome þenne,

1384"For by a-corde of couenaunt 3e craue hit as your awen."
"Þis is soth," quod þe segge, "I say yow þatilke,
& I haf worthyly þis wone3 wyth-inne,
I-wysse with as god wylle hit worþe3 to 3oure3."

1388He hasppe3 his fayre hals his arme3 wyth-inne,
& kysses hym as comlyly as he couþe awyse:
"Tas yow þere my cheuicaunce, I cheued no more,
I wowche hit saf fynly, þa3 feler hit were."

1392"Hit is god," quod þe god mon, "grant mercy þerfore,
Hit may be such, hit is þe better, &[1] 3e me breue wolde
Where 3e wan þis ilk wele, biwytte of hor seluen?"
"Þat wat3 not forward," quod he, "frayst me no more,

1396For 3e haftan þat yow tyde3, trawe3e non oþer
3e mowe."
Þay la3ed, & made hem blyþe,
Wyth lote3 þat were to lowe,

1400To soper þay 3ede asswyþe,
Wyth dayntes nwe in-nowe.

XI.

And syþen by þe chymné in chamber þay seten.
Wy3e3 þe walle wyn we3ed to hem oft,

$_{1404}$& efte in her bourdyng þay bayþen in þe morn,
To fylle þe same forwardeȝ þat þay by-fore maden,
Þat chaunce so bytydeȝ hor cheuysaunce to chaunge,
What nweȝ so þay nome, at naȝt quen þay metten

$_{1408}$Þay acorded of þe couenaunteȝ byfore þe court alle;
Þe beuerage watȝ broȝt forth in bourde at þat tyme;
Þenne þay louelych leȝten leue at þe last,
Vche burne to his bedde busked bylyue.

$_{1412}$Bi þat þe coke hade croweȝ & cakled bot þryse,
Þe lorde watȝ lopen of his bedde, [&] þe leudeȝ vch one,
So þat þe mete & þe masse watȝ metely delyuered;
Þe douthe dressed to þe wod, er any day sprenged,

$_{1416}$to chace;
Heȝ with hunte & horneȝ,
Þurȝ playneȝ þay passe in space,
Vn-coupled among þo þorneȝ,

$_{1420}$Racheȝ þat ran on race.

XII.

Sone þay calle of a quest in aker syde,
Þe hunt re-hayted þe houndeȝ, þat hit fyrst mynged,
Wylde wordeȝ hym warp wyth a wrast noyce;

$_{1424}$Þe howndeȝ þat hit herde, hastid þider swyþe,
& fellen as fast to þe fuyt, fourty at ones;
Þenne such a glauerande glam of gedered rachcheȝ
Ros, þat þe rochereȝ rungen aboute;

$_{1428}$Huntereȝ hem hardened with horne & wyth muthe.
Þen al in a semblé sweyed to-geder,
Bitwene a flosche in þat fryth, & a foo cragge;

In a knot, bi a clyffe, at þe kerre syde,

1432Þer as þe rogh rocher vn-rydely watȝ fallen,
[Þay] ferden to þe fyndyng, & frekeȝ hem after;
Þay vmbe-kesten þe knarre & þe knot boþe.
Wyȝeȝ, whyl þay wysten wel wyt inne hem hit were,

1436Þe best þat þer breued watȝ wyth þe blod houndeȝ.
Þenne þay beten on þe buskeȝ, & bede hym vp ryse,
& he vnsoundyly out soȝt seggeȝ ouer-þwert,
On þe sellokest swyn swenged out þere,

1440Long sythen for þe sounder þat wiȝt for-olde,
For he watȝ b[este &] bor alþer grattest,
[And eue]re quen he gronyed, þenne greued mony,
For [þre a]t þe fyrst þrast he þryȝt to þe erþe,

1444& [sped hym] forth good sped, boute spyt more,
[Ande þay] halowed hyghe ful hyȝe & hay! hay! cryed
Haden horneȝ to mouþe heterly rechated;
Mony watȝ þe myry mouthe of men & of houndeȝ,

1448Þat buskkeȝ after þis bor, with bost & wyth noyse,
To quelle;
Ful oft he bydeȝ þe baye,
& maymeȝ þe mute Inn-melle,

1452He hurteȝ of þe houndeȝ, & þay
Ful ȝomerly ȝaule & ȝelle.

XIII.

Schalkeȝ to schote at hym schowen to þenne,
Haled to hym of her areweȝ, hitten hym oft;

1456Bot þe poynteȝ payred at þe pyth þat pyȝt in his scheldeȝ,

& þe barbeȝ of his browe bite non wolde,
Þaȝ þe schauen schaft schyndered in peceȝ,
Þe hede hypped aȝayn, were-so-euer hit hitte;

₁₄₆₀Bot quon þe dynteȝ hym dered of her dryȝe strokeȝ,
Þen, brayn-wod for bate, on burneȝ he raseȝ,
Hurteȝ hem ful heterly þer he forth hyȝeȝ,
& mony arȝed þerat, & on-lyte droȝen.

₁₄₆₄Bot þe lorde on a lyȝt horce launces hym after,
As burne bolde vpon bent his bugle he bloweȝ,
He rechated, & r[ode] þurȝ roneȝ ful þyk,
Suande þis wy[ld]e swyn til þe sunne schafted.

₁₄₆₈Þis day wyth þis ilk dede þay dryuen on þis wyse,
Whyle oure luflych lede lys in his bedde,
Gawayn grayþely at home, in gereȝ ful ryche
of hewe;

₁₄₇₂Þe lady noȝt forȝate,
Com to hym to salue,
Ful erly ho watȝ hym ate,
His mode forto remwe.

XIV.

₁₄₇₆Ho commes to þe cortyn, & at þe knyȝt totes,
Sir Wawen her welcumed worþy on fyrst,
& ho hym ȝeldeȝ aȝayn, ful ȝerne of hir wordeȝ,
Setteȝ hir sof[t]ly by his syde, & swyþely ho laȝeȝ,

₁₄₈₀& wyth a luflych loke ho layde hym þyse wordeȝ:
"Sir, ȝif ȝe be Wawen, wonder me þynkkeȝ,
Wyȝe þat is so wel wrast alway to god,
& conneȝ not of compaynye þe costeȝ vnder-take,

60

₁₄₈₄& if mon kennes yow hom to knowe, ȝe kest hom of your
 mynde;
Þou hatȝ for-ȝeten ȝederly þat ȝisterday I taȝtte
alder-truest token of talk þat I cowþe."
"What is þat?" quod þe wyghe, "I-wysse I wot neuer,

₁₄₈₈If hit be sothe þat ȝe breue, þe blame is myn awen."
"ȝet I kende yow of kyssyng," quod þe clere þenne,
"Quere-so countenaunce is couþe, quikly to clayme,
Þat bicumes vche a knyȝt, þat cortaysy vses."

₁₄₉₂"Do way," quod þat derf mon, "my dere, þat speche,
For þat durst I not do, lest I denayed were,
If I were werned, I were wrang I-wysse, ȝif I profered."
"Ma fay," quod þe mere wyf, "ȝe may not be werned,

₁₄₉₆ȝe ar stif in-noghe to constrayne wyth strenkþe, ȝif yow
 lykeȝ,
ȝif any were so vilanous þat yow denaye wolde."
"ȝe, be God," quod Gawayn, "good is your speche,
Bot þrete is vn-þryuande in þede þer I lende,

₁₅₀₀& vche gift þat is geuen not with goud wylle;
I am at your comaundement, to kysse quen yow lykeȝ,
ȝe may lach quen yow lyst, & leue quen yow þynkkeȝ,
 in space."

₁₅₀₄Þe lady louteȝ a-doun,
& comlyly kysses his face,
Much speche þay þer expoun,
Of druryes greme & grace.

V.

₁₅₀₈"I woled wyt at yow, wyȝe," þat worþy þer sayde,
"& yow wrathed not þer-wyth, what were þe skylle,

Þat so ȝong & so ȝepe, as ȝe [ar] at þis tyme,
So cortayse, so knyȝtyly, as ȝe ar knowen oute,

1512& of alle cheualry to chose, þe chef þyng a-losed,
Is² þe lel layk of luf, þe lettrure of armes;
F[or] to telle of þis tenelyng of þis trwe knyȝteȝ,
Hit is þe tytelet, token, & tyxt of her werkkeȝ,

1516How le[des] for her lele luf hor lyueȝ han auntered,
Endured for her drury dulful stoundeȝ,
& after wenged with her walour & voyded her care,
& broȝt blysse in-to boure, with bountees hor awen.

1520& ȝe ar knyȝt com-lokest kyd of your elde,
Your worde & your worchip walkeȝ ay quere,
& I haf seten by your-self here sere twyes,
ȝet herde I neuer of your hed helde no wordeȝ

1524Þat euer longed to luf, lasse ne more;
& ȝe, þat ar so cortays & coynt of your hetes,
Oghe to a ȝonke þynk ȝern to schewe,
& teche sum tokeneȝ of trweluf craftes.

1528Why ar ȝe lewed, þat alle þe los weldeȝ,
Oþer elles ȝe demen me to dille, your dalyaunce to herken?
for schame!
I com hider sengel, & sitte,

1532To lerne at yow sum game,
Dos, techeȝ me of your wytte,
Whil my lorde is fro hame."

XVI.

"In goud fayþe," quod Gawayn, "God yow forȝelde,

₁₅₃₆Gret is þe gode gle, & gomen to me huge,
Þat so worþy as ȝe wolde wynne hidere,
& pyne yow with so pouer a mon, as play wyth your knyȝt,
With any skynneȝ countenaunce, hit keuereȝ me ese;

₁₅₄₀Bot to take þe toruayle to my-self, to trwluf expoun,
& towche þe temeȝ of tyxt, & taleȝ of armeȝ,
To yow þat, I wot wel, weldeȝ more slyȝt
Of þat art, bi þe half, or a hundreth of seche

₁₅₄₄As I am, oþer euer schal, in erde þer I leue,
Hit were a fole fele-folde, my fre, by my trawþe.
I wolde yowre wylnyng worche at my myȝt,
As I am hyȝly bihalden, & euer-more wylle

₁₅₄₈Be seruaunt to your-seluen, so saue me dryȝtyn!"
Þus hym frayned þat fre, & fondet hym ofte,
Forto haf wonnen hym to woȝe, what-so scho þoȝt elleȝ,
Bot he de fended hym so fayr, þat no faut semed,

₁₅₅₂Ne non euel on nawþer halue, nawþer þay wysten,
bot blysse;
Þay laȝed & layked longe,
At þe last scho con hym kysse,

₁₅₅₆Hir leue fayre con scho fonge,
& went hir waye Iwysse.

XVII.

Then ruþes hym þe renk, & ryses to þe masse,
& siþen hor diner watȝ dyȝt & derely serued.

₁₅₆₀Þe lede with þe ladyeȝ layked alle day,
Bot þe lorde ouer þe londeȝ launced ful ofte,
Sweȝ his vncely swyn, þat swyngeȝ bi þe bonkkeȝ,

& bote þe best of his brache3 þe bakke3 in sunder;

1564Þer he bode in his bay, tel bawe-men hit breken,
& made hym, maw-gref his bed, forto mwe vtter;
So felle flone3 per flete, when þe folk gedered;
Bot 3et þe styffest to start bi stounde3 he made,

1568Til at þe last he wat3 so mat, he my3t no more renne,
Bot in þe hast þat he my3t, he to a hole wynne3,
Of a rasse, bi a rokk, þer renne3 þe boerne,
He gete þe bonk at his bak, bigyne3 to scrape,

1572Þe froþe femed at his mouth vnfayre bi þe wyke3,
Whette3 his whyte tusche3; with hym þen irked
Alle þe burne3 so bolde, þat hym by stoden,
To nye hym on-ferum, bot ne3e hym non durst

1576for woþe;
He hade hurt so mony byforne,
Þat al þu3t þenne ful loþe,
Be more wyth his tusche3 torne,

1580Þat breme wat3 [&] brayn-wod bothe.

XVIII.

Til þe kny3t com hym-self, kachande his blonk,
Sy3 hym byde at þe bay, his burne3 bysyde,
He ly3tes luflych adoun, leue3 his corsour,

1584Brayde3 out a bry3t bront, & bigly forth stryde3,
Founde3 fast þur3 þe forth, þer þe felle byde3,
Þe wylde wat3 war of þe wy3e with weppen in honde,
Hef hy3ly þe here, so hetterly he fnast,

1588Þat fele ferde for þe freke3, lest felle hym þe worre;

64

Þe swyn setteӡ hym out on þe segge euen,
Þat þe burne & þe bor were boþe vpon hepeӡ,
In þe wyӡt-est of þe water, þe worre hade þat oþer;

1592For þe mon merkkeӡ hym wel, as þay mette fyrst,
Set sadly þe scharp in þe slot euen,
Hit hym vp to þe hult, þat þe hert schyndered,
& he ӡarrande hym ӡelde, & ӡedoun³ þe water,

1596ful tyt;
A hundreth houndeӡ hym hent,
Þat bremely con hym bite,
Burneӡ him broӡt to bent,

1600& doggeӡ to dethe endite.

XIX.

There watӡ blawyng of prys in mony breme home,
Heӡe halowing on hiӡe, with haþeleӡ þat myӡt;
Brachetes bayed þat best, as bidden þe maystereӡ,

1604Of þat chargeaunt chace þat were chef huntes.
Þenne a wyӡe þat watӡ wys vpon wod crafteӡ,
To vnlace þis bor lufly bigynneӡ;
Fyrst he hewes of his hed, & on hiӡe setteӡ,

1608& syþen rendeӡ him al roghe bi þe rygge after,
Braydeӡ out þe boweles, brenneӡ hom on glede,
With bred blent þer-with his braches rewardeӡ;
Syþen he britneӡ out þe brawen in bryӡt brode [s]cheldeӡ,

1612& hatӡ out þe hastletteӡ, as hiӡtly bisemeӡ;
& ӡet hem halcheӡ al hole þe halueӡ to-geder,
& syþen on a stif stange stoutly hem henges.
Now with þis ilk swyn þay swengen to home;

₁₆₁₆Þe bores hed watȝ borne bifore þe burnes seluen,
Þat him for-ferde in þe forþe, þurȝ forse of his honde,
so stronge;
Til he seȝ sir Gawayne,

₁₆₂₀In halle hym þoȝt ful longe,
He calde, & he com gayn,
His feeȝ þer for to fonge.

XX.

Þe lorde ful lowde with lote, & laȝed myry,

₁₆₂₄When he seȝe sir G: with solace he spekeȝ;
Þe goude ladyeȝ were geten, & gedered þe meyny,
He scheweȝ hem þe scheldeȝ, & schapes hem þe tale,
Of þe largesse, & þe lenþe, þe liþerneȝ alse,

₁₆₂₈Of þe were of þe wylde swyn, in wod þer he fled.
Þat oþer knyȝt ful comly comended his dedeȝ,
& praysed hit as gret prys, þat he proued hade;
For suche a brawne of a best, þe bolde burne sayde,

₁₆₃₂Ne such sydes of a swyn, segh he neuer are.
Þenne hondeled þay þe hoge hed, þe hende mon hit praysed,
& let lodly þerat þe lorde forte here:
"Now Gawayn," quod þe god mon, "þis gomen is your awen,

₁₆₃₆Bi fyn for-warde & faste, faythely ȝe knowe."
"Hit is sothe," quod þe segge, "& as siker trwe;
Alle my get I schal yow gif agayn, bi my trawþe."
He [hent] þe haþel aboute þe halse, & hendely hym kysses,

₁₆₄₀& efter-sones of þe same he serued hym þere.
"Now ar we euen," quod þe haþel, "in þis euen-tide,
Of alle þe couenauntes þat we knyt, syþen I com hider,

bi lawe;"

₁₆₄₄Þe lorde sayde, "bi saynt Gile,
ȝe ar þe best þat I knowe,
ȝe ben ryche in a whyle,
Such chaffer & ȝe drowe."

XI.

₁₆₄₈Þenne þay teldet tableȝ [on] trestes alofte,
Kesten cloþeȝ vpon, clere lyȝt þenne
Wakned bi woȝeȝ, waxen torches
Seggeȝ sette, & serued in sale al aboute;

₁₆₅₂Much glam & gle glent vp þer-inne,
Aboute þe fyre vpon flet, & on fele wyse,
At þe soper & after, mony aþel songeȝ,
As coundutes of kryst-masse, & caroleȝ newe,

₁₆₅₆With alle þe manerly merþe þat mon may of telle.
& euer oure luflych knyȝt þe lady bi-syde;
Such semblaunt to þat segge semly ho made,
Wyth stille stollen countenaunce, þat stalworth to plese,

₁₆₆₀Þat al for-wondered watȝ þe wyȝe, & wroth with hym-seluen,
Bot he nolde not for his nurture nurne hir a-ȝayneȝ,
Bot dalt with hir al in daynte, how-se-euer þe dede turned
to wrast;

₁₆₆₄Quen þay hade played in halle,
As longe as hor wylle hom last,
To chambre he con hym calle,
& to þe chem-ne þay past.

67

XXII.

₁₆₆₈Ande þer þay dronken, & dalten, & demed eft nwe,
To norne on þe same note, on nweȝereȝ euen;
Bot þe knyȝt craued leue, to kayre on þe morn,
For hit watȝ neȝ at þe terme, þat he to schulde.

₁₆₇₂Þe lorde hym letted of þat, to lenge hym resteyed,
& sayde, "as I am trwe segge, I siker my trawþe,
Þou schal cheue to þe grene chapel, þy charres to make,
Leude, on nwȝereȝ lyȝt, longe bifore pryme:

₁₆₇₆For-þy þow lye in þy loft, & lach þyn ese,
& I schal hunt in þis holt, & halde þe towcheȝ,
Chaunge wyth þe cheuisaunce, bi þat I charre hider;
For I haf fraysted þe twys, & faythful I fynde þe,

₁₆₈₀Now þrid tyme þrowe best þenk on þe morne,
Make we mery quyl we may, & mynne vpon Ioye,
For þe lur may mon lach, when so mon lykeȝ."
Þis watȝ grayþely graunted, & Gawayn is lenged,

₁₆₈₄Bliþe broȝt watȝ hym drynk, & þay to bedde ȝeden,
with liȝt;
Sir G: lis & slepes,
Ful stille & softe al niȝt;

₁₆₈₈Þe lorde þat his crafteȝ kepes,
Ful erly he watȝ diȝt.

XXIII.

After messe a morsel he & his men token,
Miry watȝ þe mornyng, his mounture he askes;

1692Alle þe haþeles þat on horse schulde helden hym after,
Were boun busked on hor blonkkeȝ, bi-fore þe halle ȝateȝ;
Ferly fayre watȝ þe folde, for þe forst clenged,
In rede rudede vpon rak rises þe sunne,

1696& ful clere costeȝ þe clowdes of þe welkyn.
Hunteres vnhardeled bi a holt syde,
Rocheres roungen bi rys, for rurde of her hornes;
Summe fel in þe fute, þer þe fox bade,

1700Trayleȝ ofte a trayteres, bi traunt of her wyles;
A kenet kryes þerof, þe hunt on hym calles,
His felaȝes fallen hym to, þat fnasted ful þike,
Runnen forth in a rabel, in his ryȝt fare;

1704& he fyskeȝ hem by-fore, þay founden hym sone,
& quen þay seghe hym with syȝt, þay sued hym fast,
Wreȝande h[ym] ful [w]eterly with a wroth noyse;
& he trantes & tornayeeȝ þurȝ mony tene greue;

1708Hamlouneȝ, & herkeneȝ, bi heggeȝ ful ofte;
At þe last bi a littel dich he lepeȝ ouer a spenné,
Steleȝ out ful stilly bi a strothe rande,
Went haf wylt of þe wode, with wyleȝ fro þe houndes,

1712Þenne watȝ he went, er he wyst, to a wale tryster,
Þer þre þro at a þrich þrat hym at ones,
al graye;
He blenched aȝayn bilyue,

1716& stifly start onstray,
With alle þe wo on lyue,
To þe wod he went away.

XXIV.

Thenne wat3 hit lif vpon list to lyþen þe hounde3,

1720When alle þe mute hade hym met, menged to-geder,
Suche a sor3e at þat sy3t þay sette on his hede,
As alle þe clamberande clyffes hade clatered on hepes;
Here he wat3 halawed, when haþele3 hym metten,

1724Loude he wat3 3ayned, with 3arande speche;
Þer he wat3 þreted, & ofte þef called,
& ay þe titleres at his tayl, þat tary he ne my3t;
Ofte he wat3 runnen at, when he out rayked,

1728& ofte reled in a3ayn, so reniarde wat3 wylé.
& 3e he lad hem bi lag, mon, þe lorde & his meyny;
On þis maner bi þe mountes, quyle myd, ouer, vnder,
Meanwhile the knight at home soundly sleeps within his comely
    curtains.
Whyle þe hende kny3t at home holsumly slepe3,

1732With-inne þe comly cortynes, on þe colde morne.
Bot þe lady for luf let not to slepe,
Ne þe purpose to payre, þat py3t in hir hert,
Bot ros hir vp radly, rayked hir þeder,

1736In a mery mantyle, mete to þe erþe,
Þat wat3 furred ful fyne with felle3, wel pured,
No hwe3 goud on hir hede, bot þe ha3er stones
Trased aboute hir tressour, be twenty in clusteres;

1740Hir þryuen face & hir þrote þrowen al naked,
Hir brest bare bifore, & bihinde eke.
Ho come3 with-inne þe chambre dore, & closes hit hir after,
Wayne3 vp a wyndow, & on þe wy3e calle3,

₁₇₄₄& radly þus re-hayted hym, with hir riche worde₃,
with chere;
"A! mon, how may þou slepe,
Þis morning is so clere?"

₁₇₄₈He wat₃ in drowping depe,
Bot þenne he con hir here.

XXV.

In dre₃ droupyng of dreme draueled þat noble,
As mon þat wat₃ in mornyng of mony þro þo₃tes,

₁₇₅₂How þat destiné schulde þat day [dy₃t] his wyrde,
At þe grene chapel, when he þe gome metes,
& bi-houes his buffet abide, with-oute debate more;
Bot quen þat comly he keuered his wyttes,

₁₇₅₆Swenges out of þe sweuenes, & sware₃ with hast.
Þe lady luflych com la₃ande swete,
Felle ouer his fayre face, & fetly him kyssed;
He welcume₃ hir worþily, with a wale chere;

₁₇₆₀He se₃ hir so glorious, & gayly atyred,
So fautles of hir fetures, & of so fyne hewes,
Wi₃t wallande Ioye warmed his hert;
With smoþe smylyng & smolt þay smeten in-to merþe,

₁₇₆₄Þat al wat₃ blis & bonchef, þat breke hem bi-twene,
& wynne,
Þay lanced wordes gode,
Much wele þen wat₃ þer-inne,

₁₇₆₈Gret perile bi-twene hem stod,
Nif mare of hir kny₃t mynne.

XXVI.

For þat prynce of pris de-presed hym so þikke.
Nurned hym so neȝe þe þred, þat nede hym bi-houed,

1772Oþer lach þer hir luf, oþer lodly re-fuse;
He cared for his cortaysye, lest craþayn he were,
& more for his meschef, ȝif he schulde make synne,
& be traytor to þat tolke, þat þat telde aȝt.

1776"God schylde," quod þe schalk, "þat schal not be-falle!"
With luf-laȝyng a lyt, he layd hym by-syde
Alle þe specheȝ of specialté þat sprange of her mouthe.
Quod þat burde to þe burne, "blame ȝe disserue,

1780ȝif ȝe luf not þat lyf þat ȝe lye nexte,
Bifore alle þe wyȝeȝ in þe worlde, wounded in hert,
Bot if ȝe haf a lemman, a leuer, þat yow lykeȝ better,
& folden fayth to þat fre, festned so harde,

1784Þat yow lausen ne lyst, & þat I leue nouþe;
And þat ȝe telle me þat, now trwly I pray yow,
For alle þe lufeȝ vpon lyue, layne not þe soþe,
for gile."

1788Þe knyȝt sayde, "be sayn Ion,"
& smeþely con he smyle,
"In fayth I welde riȝt non,
Ne non wil welde þe quile."

XXVII.

1792"Þat is a worde," quod þat wyȝt, "þat worst is of alle,
Bot I am swared for soþe, þat sore me þinkkeȝ;
Kysse me now coraly, & I schal cach heþen,

I may bot mourne vpon molde, as may þat much louyes."

₁₇₉₆Sykande ho sweȝe doun, & semly hym kyssed,
& siþen ho seueres hym fro, & says as ho stondes,
"Now, dere, at þis de-partyng, do me þis ese,
Gif me sumquat of þy gifte, þi gloue if hit were,

₁₈₀₀Þat I may mynne on þe mon, my mournyng to lassen."
"Now Iwysse," quod þat wyȝe, "I wolde I hade here
Þe leuest þing for þy luf, þat I in londe welde,
For ȝe haf deserued, forsoþe, sellyly ofte

₁₈₀₄More rewarde bi resoun, þen I reche myȝt,
Bot to dele yow for drurye, þat dawed bot neked;
Hit is not your honour to haf at þis tyme
A gloue for a garysoun, of Gawayneȝ gifteȝ,

₁₈₀₈& I am here [on] an erande in erdeȝ vncouþe,
& haue no men wyth no maleȝ, with menskful þingeȝ;
Þat mislykeȝ me, ladé, for luf at þis tyme,
Iche tolke mon do as he is tan, tas to non ille,

₁₈₁₂ne pine."
"Nay, hende of hyȝe honours,"
Quod þat lufsum vnder lyne,
"Þaȝ I hade oȝt of youreȝ,

₁₈₁₆ȝet schulde ȝe haue of myne."

XVIII.

Ho raȝt hym a riche rynk of red golde werkeȝ,
Wyth a starande ston, stondande alofte,
Þat bere blusschande bemeȝ as þe bryȝt sunne;

₁₈₂₀Wyt ȝe wel, hit watȝ worth wele ful hoge.

73

Bot þe renk hit renayed, & redyly he sayde,
"I wil no gifteȝ for gode, my gay, at þis tyme;
I haf none yow to norne, ne noȝt wyl I take."

1824Ho bede hit hym ful bysily, & he hir bode wernes,
& swere swyftel[y] his sothe, þat he hit sese nolde;
& ho sore þat he forsoke, & sayde þer-after,
"If ȝe renay my rynk, to ryche for hit semeȝ,

1828Ȝe wolde not so hyȝly halden be to me,
I schal gif yow my girdel, þat gaynes yow lasse."
Ho laȝt a lace lyȝtly, þat leke vmbe hir sydeȝ,
Knit vpon hir kyrtel, vnder þe clere mantyle,

1832Gered hit watȝ with grene sylke, & with golde schaped,
Noȝt bot arounde brayden, beten with fyngreȝ;
& þat ho bede to þe burne, & blyþely bi-soȝt
Þaȝ hit vn-worþi were, þat he hit take wolde.

1836& he nay þat he nolde neghe in no wyse,
Nauþer golde ne garysoun, er God hym grace sende,
To acheue to þe chaunce þat he hade chosen þere.
"& þerfore, I pray yow, displese yow noȝt,

1840& letteȝ be your bisinesse, for I bayþe hit yow neuer
to graunte;
I am derely to yow biholde,
Bi-cause of your sembelaunt,

1844& euer in hot & colde
To be your trwe seruaunt.

XXIX.

"Now forsake ȝe þis silke." sayde þe burde þenne,
"For hit is symple in hit-self. & so hit wel semeȝ?

₁₈₄₈Lo! so hit is littel, & lasse hit is worþy;
Bot who-so knew þe costes þat knit ar þer-inne,
He wolde hit prayse at more prys, parauenture;
For quat gome so is gorde with þis grene lace,

₁₈₅₂While he hit hade hemely halched aboute,
Þer is no haþel vnder heuen to-hewe hym þat my3t;
For he my3t not he slayn, for sly3t vpon erþe."
Þen kest þe kny3t, & hit come to his hert,

₁₈₅₆Hit were a Iuel for þe Iopardé, þat hym iugged were,
When he acheued to þe chapel, his chek forto fech;
My3 he haf slypped to þe vn-slayn, þe sle3t were noble.
Þenne ho þulged with hir þrepe, & þoled hir to speke,

₁₈₆₀& ho bere on hym þe belt, & bede hit hym swyþe,
& he granted, & [ho] hym gafe with a goud wylle,
& biso3t hym, for hir sake, disceuer hit neuer,
Bot to lelly layne for hir lorde; þe leude hym acorde3.

₁₈₆₄Þat neuer wy3e schulde hit wyt, Iwysse, bot þay twayne,
for no3te;
He þonkked hir oft ful swyþe,
Ful þro with hert & þo3t.

₁₈₆₈Bi þat on þrynne syþe,
He hat3 kyst þe kny3t so to3t.

XXX.

Thenne lachche3 ho hir leue, & leue3 hym þere,
For more myrþe of þat mon mo3t ho not gete;

₁₈₇₂When ho wat3 gon, sir G. gere3 hym sone,
Rises, & riches hym in araye noble,
Lays vp þe luf-lace, þe lady hym ra3t,

Hid hit ful holdely, þer he hit eft fonde;

1876Syþen cheuely to þe chapel choses he þe waye,
Preuely aproched to a prest, & prayed hym þere
Þat he wolde lyfte his lyf, & lern hym better,
How his sawle schulde be saued, when he schuld seye heþen.

1880Þere he schrof hym schyrly, & schewed his mysdedeȝ,
Of þe more & þe mynne, & merci besecheȝ,
& of absolucioun he on þe segge calles;
& he asoyled hym surely, & sette hym so clene,

1884As domeȝ-day schulde haf ben diȝt on þe morn.
& syþen he mace hym as mery among þe fre ladyes,
With comlych caroles, & alle kynnes ioye,
As neuer he did bot þat daye, to þe derk nyȝt,

1888with blys;
Vche mon hade daynte þare,
Of hym, & sayde Iwysse,
Þus myry he watȝ neuer are,

1892Syn he com hider, er þis.

XXXI.

Now hym lenge iṅ þat lee, þer luf hym bi-tyde;
ȝet is þe lorde on þe launde, ledande his gomnes,
He hatȝ forfaren þis fox, þat he folȝed longe;

1896As he sprent ouer a spenné, to spye þe schrewe,
Þer as he herd þe howndes, þat hasted hym swyþe,
Renaud com richchande þurȝ a roȝe greue,
& alle þe rabel in a res, ryȝt at his heleȝ.

1900Þe wyȝe watȝ war of þe wylde, & warly abides,

& brayde3 out þe bry3t bronde, & at þe best caste3;
& he schunt for þe scharp, & schulde haf arered,
A rach rapes hym to, ry3t er he my3t,

1904& ry3t bifore þe hors fete þay fel on hym alle,
& woried me þis wyly wyth a wroth noyse.
Þe lorde ly3te3 bilyue, & cache3 by sone,
Rased hym ful radly out of þe rach mouþes,

1908Halde3 he3e ouer his hede, halowe3 faste,
& þer bayen hym mony bray hounde3;
Huntes hy3ed hem þeder, with horne3 ful mony,
Ay re-chatande ary3t til þay þe renk se3en;

1912Bi þat wat3 comen his compeyny noble,
Alle þat euer ber bugle blowed at ones,
& alle þise oþer halowed, þat hade no hornes,
Hit wat3 þe myriest mute þat euer men herde,

1916Þe rich rurd þat þer wat3 raysed for renaude saule,
with lote;
Hor hounde3 þay þer rewarde,
Her hede3 þay fawne & frote,

1920& syþen þay tan reynarde,
& tyrnen of his cote.

XXXII.

& þenne þay helden to home, for hit wat3 nie3 ny3t,
Strakande ful stoutly in hor store horne3;

1924Þe lorde is ly3t at þe laste at hys lef home,
Fynde3 fire vpon flet, þe freke þer by-side,
Sir Gawayn þe gode, þat glad wat3 with alle,
Among þe ladies for luf he ladde much ioye,

₁₉₂₈He were a bleaunt of blwe, þat bradde to þe erþe,
His surkot semed hym wel, þat softe watȝ forred,
& his hode of þat ilke henged on his schulder,
Blande al of blaunner were boþe al aboute.

₁₉₃₂He meteȝ me þis god mon in myddeȝ þe flore,
& al with gomen he hym gret, & goudly he sayde,
"I schal fylle vpon fyrst oure forwardeȝ nouþe,
Þat we spedly han spoken, þer spared watȝ no drynk;"

₁₉₃₆Þen acoles he [þe] knyȝt, & kysses hym þryes,
As sauerly & sadly as he hem sette couþe.
"Bi Kryst," quod þat oþer knyȝt, "ȝe cach much sele,
In cheuisaunce of þis chaffer, ȝif ȝe hade goud chepeȝ."

₁₉₄₀"Ȝe of þe chepe no charg," quod chefly þat oþer,
"As is pertly payed þe chepeȝ þat I aȝte."
"Mary," quod þat oþer mon, "myn is bi-hynde,
For I haf hunted al þis day, & noȝt haf I geten,

₁₉₄₄Bot þis foule fox felle, þe fende haf þe godeȝ,
& þat is ful pore, for to pay for suche prys þinges,
As ȝe haf þryȝt me here, þro suche þre cosses,
so gode."

₁₉₄₈"I-noȝ," quod sir Gawayn,
"I þonk yow, bi þe rode;"
& how þe fox watȝ slayn,
He tolde hym, as þay stode.

XXXIII.

₁₉₅₂With merþe & mynstralsye, wyth meteȝ at hor wylle,
Þay maden as mery as any men moȝten,
With laȝyng of ladies, with loteȝ of bordes;
Gawayn & þe gode mon so glad were þay boþe,

1956Bot if þe douthe had doted, oþer dronken ben oþer,
Boþe þe mon & þe meyny maden mony iapeȝ,
Til þe sesoun watȝ seȝen, þat þay seuer moste;
Burneȝ to hor bedde be-houed at þe laste.

1960Þenne loȝly his leue at þe lorde fyrst
Fochcheȝ þis fre mon, & fayre he hym þonkkeȝ;
"Of such a sellyly soiorne, as I haf hade here,
Your honour, at þis hyȝe fest, þe hyȝe kyng yow ȝelde!

1964I ȝef yow me for on of youreȝ, if yowre-self lykeȝ,
For I mot nedes, as ȝe wot, meue to morne;
& ȝe me take sum tolke, to teche, as ȝe hyȝt,
Þe gate to þe grene chapel, as god wyl me suffer

1968To dele, on nwȝereȝ day, þe dome of my wyrdes."
"In god fayþe," quod þe god mon. "wyth a goud wylle;
Al þat euer I yow hyȝt, halde schal I rede."
Þer asyngnes he a seruaunt, to sett hym in þe waye,

1972& coundue hym by þe downeȝ, þat he no drechch had,
For to f[e]rk þurȝ þe fryth, & fare at þe gaynest,
bi greue.
Þe lorde Gawayn con þonk,

1976Such worchip he wolde hym weue;
Þen at þo ladyeȝ wlonk.
Þe knyȝt hatȝ tan his leue.

XXIV.

With care & wyth kyssyng he carppeȝ hem tille,

1980& fele þryuande þonkkeȝ he þrat hom to haue,
& þay ȝelden hym aȝay[n] ȝeply þat ilk;
Þay bikende hym to Kryst, with ful colde sykyngeȝ.

Syþen fro þe meyny he menskly de-partes;

₁₉₈₄Vche mon þat he mette, he made hem a þonke,
For his seruyse, & his solace, & his sere pyne,
Þat þay wyth busynes had ben, aboute hym to serue;
& vche segge as sore, to seuer with hym þere,

₁₉₈₈As þay hade wonde worþyly with þat wlonk euer.
Þen with ledes & lyȝt he watȝ ladde to his chambre,
& blybely broȝt to his bedde, to be at his rest;
ȝif he ne slepe soundyly, say ne dar I,

₁₉₉₂For he hade muche on þe morn to mynne, ȝif he wolde,
in þoȝt;
Let hym lyȝe þere stille,
He hatȝ nere þat he soȝt,

₁₉₉₆& ȝe wyl a whyle be stylle,
I schal telle yow how þay wroȝt.

FYTTE THE FOURTH

I.

Now neȝeȝ þe nwȝere, & þe nyȝt passeȝ,
Þe day dryueȝ to þe derk, as dryȝtyn biddeȝ;

2000Bot wylde wedereȝ of þe worlde wakned þeroute,
Clowdes kesten kenly þe colde to þe erþe,
Wyth nyȝe in-noghe of þe norþe, þe naked to tene;
Þe snawe snitered ful snart, þat snayped þe wylde;

2004Þe werbelande wynde wapped fro þe hyȝe,
& drof vche dale ful of dryftes ful grete.
Þe leude lystened ful wel, þat leȝ in his bedde,
Þaȝ he lowkeȝ his liddeȝ, ful lyttel he slepes;

2008Bi vch kok þat crue, he knwe wel þe steuen.
De-liuerly he dressed vp, er þe day sprenged,
For þere watȝ lyȝt of a lau[m]pe, þat lemed in his chambre;
He called to his chamberlayn, þat cofly hym swared,

$_{2012}$& bede hym bryng hym his bruny, & his blonk sadel;
Þat oþer ferkeȝ hym vp, & fecheȝ hym his wedeȝ,
& grayþeȝ me sir Gawayn vpon a grett wyse.
Fyrst he clad hym in his cloþeȝ, þe colde for to were;

$_{2016}$& syþen his oþer harnays, þat holdely watȝ keped,
Boþe his paunce, & his plateȝ, piked ful clene,
Þe ryngeȝ rokked of þe roust, of his riche bruny;
& al watȝ fresch as vpon fyrst, & he watȝ fayn þenne

$_{2020}$to þonk;
He hade vpon vche pece,
Wypped ful wel & wlonk;
Þe gayest in to Grece,

$_{2024}$Þe burne bede bryng his blonk.

II.

Whyle þe wlonkest wedes he warp on hym-seluen;
His cote, wyth be conysaunce of þe clere werkeȝ,
Ennurned vpon veluet vertuuus stoneȝ,

$_{2028}$Aboute beten, & bounden, enbrauded semeȝ,
& fayre furred with-inne wyth fayre pelures.
ȝet laft he not þe lace, þe ladieȝ gifte,
Þat for-gat not Gawayn, for gode of hym-seluen;

$_{2032}$Bi he hade belted þe bronde vpon his balȝe hauncheȝ,
Þenn dressed he his drurye double hym aboute;
Swyþe sweþled vmbe his swange swetely, þat knyȝt,
Þe gordel of þe grene silke, þat gay wel bisemed,

$_{2036}$Vpon þat ryol red cloþe, þat ryche watȝ to schewe.
Bot wered not þis ilk wyȝe for wele þis gordel,
For pryde of þe pendaunteȝ, þaȝ polyst þay were,

& þaȝ þe glyterande golde glent vpon endeȝ,

2040Bot forto sauen hym-self, when suffer hym by-houed,
To byde bale with-oute dabate, of bronde hym to were,
oþer knyffe;
Bi þat þe bolde mon boun,

2044Wynneȝ þeroute bilyue,
Alle þe meyny of renoun,
He þonkkeȝ ofte ful ryue.

III.

Thenne watȝ Gryngolet grayþe, þat gret watȝ & huge,

2048& hade ben soiourned sauerly, & in a siker wyse,
Hym lyst prik for poynt, þat proude hors þenne;
Þe wyȝe wynneȝ hym to, & wyteȝ on his lyre,
& sayde soberly hym-self, & by his soth swereȝ,

2052"Here is a meyny in þis mote, þat on menske þenkkeȝ,
Þe mon hem maynteines, ioy mot þay haue;
Þe leue lady, on lyue luf hir bityde;
ȝif þay for charyté cherysen a gest,

2056& halden honour in her honde, þe haþel hem ȝelde,
Þat haldeȝ þe heuen vpon hyȝe, & also yow alle!
& ȝif I myȝt lyf vpon londe lede any quyle,
I schuld rech yow sum rewarde redyly, if I myȝt."

2060Þenn steppeȝ he in-to stirop, & strydeȝ alofte;
His schalk schewed hym his schelde, on schulder he hit laȝt,
Gordeȝ to Gryngolet, with his gilt heleȝ,
& he starteȝ on þe ston, stod he no lenger,

2064to praunce;

83

His haþel on hors watȝ þenne,
Þat bere his spere & launce.
"Þis kastel to Kryst I kenne,

2068He gef hit ay god chaunce!"

IV.

The brygge watȝ brayde doun, & þe brode ȝateȝ
Vnbarred, & born open, vpon boþe halue;
Þe burne blessed hym bilyue, & þe bredeȝ passed;

2072Prayses þe porter, bifore þe prynce kneled,
Gef hym God & goud day, þat Gawayn he saue;
& went on his way, with his wyȝe one,
Þat schulde teche hym to tourne to þat tene place,

2076Þer þe ruful race he schulde re-sayue.
Þay boȝen bi bonkkeȝ, þer boȝeȝ ar bare,
Þay clomben bi clyffeȝ, þer clengeȝ þe colde;
Þe heuen watȝ vp halt, bot vgly þer vnder,

2080Mist muged on þe mor, malt on þe mounteȝ,
Vch hille hade a hatte, a myst-hakel huge;
Brokeȝ byled, & breke, bi bonkkeȝ aboute,
Schyre schaterande on schoreȝ, þer þay doun schowued.

2084Welawylle watȝ þe way, þer þay bi wod schulden,
Til hit watȝ sone sesoun, þat þe sunne ryses,
þat tyde;
Þay were on a hille ful hyȝe,

2088Þe quyte snaw lay bisyde;
Þe burne þat rod hym by
Bede his mayster abide.

"For I haf wonnen yow hider, wyȝe, at þis tyme,

2092& now nar ȝe not fer fro þat note place,
Þat ȝe han spied & spuryed so specially after;
Bot I schal say yow for soþe, syþen I yow knowe,
& ȝe ar a lede vpon lyue, þat I wel louy,

2096Wolde ȝe worch bi my wytte, ȝe worþed þe better.
Þe place þat ȝe prece to, ful perelous is halden;
Þer woneȝ a wyȝe in þat waste, þe worst vpon erþe;
For he is stiffe, & sturne, & to strike louies,

2100& more he is þen any mon vpon myddelerde,
& his body bigger þen þe best fowre.
Þat ar in Arþureȝ hous, Hestor oþer oþer.
He cheueȝ þat chaunce at þe chapel grene;

2104Þer passes non bi þat place, so proude in his armes,
Þat he ne dynneȝ hym to deþe, with dynt of his honde;
For he is a mon methles, & mercy non vses,
For be hit chorle, oþer chaplayn, þat bi þe chapel rydes,

2108Monk, oþer masse-prest, oþer any mon elles,
Hym þynk as queme hym to quelle, as quyk go hym seluen.
For-þy I say þe as soþe as ȝe in sadel sitte,
Com ȝe þere, ȝe be kylled, [I] may þe knyȝt rede,

2112Trawe ȝe me þat trwely, þaȝ ȝe had twenty lyues
to spende;
He hatȝ wonyd here ful ȝore,
On bent much baret bende,

2116Aȝayn his dynteȝ sore,
ȝe may not yow defende."

85

VI.

"For-þy, goude sir Gawayn, let þe gome one,
& gotȝ a-way sum oþer gate; vpon Goddeȝ halue;

₂₁₂₀Cayreȝ bi sum oþer kyth, þer Kryst mot yow spede;
& I schal hyȝ me hom aȝayn, & hete yow fyrre,
Þat I schal swere bi God, & alle his gode halȝeȝ,
As help me God & þe halydam, & oþeȝ in-noghe,

₂₁₂₄Þat I schal lelly yow layne, & lance neuer tale,
Þat euer ȝe fondet to fle, for freke þat I wyst."
"Grant merci;" quod Gawayn, & gruchyng he sayde,
"Wel worth þe wyȝe, þat woldeȝ my gode,

₂₁₂₈& þat lelly me layne, I leue wel þou woldeȝ!
Bot helde þou hit neuer so holde, & I here passed,
Founded for ferde for to fle, in fourme þat þou telleȝ,
I were a knyȝt kowarde, I myȝt not be excused.

₂₁₃₂Bot I wyl to þe chapel, for chaunce þat may falle,
& talk wyth þat ilk tulk þe tale þat me lyste,
Worþe hit wele, oþer wo, as þe wyrde lykeȝ
hit hafe;

₂₁₃₆Þaȝe he be a sturn knape,
To stiȝtel, & stad with staue,
Ful wel con dryȝtyn schape,
His seruaunteȝ forto saue."

VII.

₂₁₄₀"Mary!" quod þat oþer mon, "now þou so much spelleȝ,
Þat þou wylt þyn awen nye nyme to þy-seluen,
& þe lyst lese þy lyf, þe lette I ne kepe;

Haf here þi helme on þy hede, þi spere in þi honde,

₂₁₄₄& ryde me doun þis ilk rake, bi ȝon rokke syde,
Til þou be broȝt to þe boþem of þe brem valay;
Þenne loke a littel on þe launde, on þi lyfte honde,
& þou schal se in þat slade þe self chapel,

₂₁₄₈& þe borelych burne on bent, þat hit kepeȝ.
Now fareȝ wel on Godeȝ half, Gawayn þe noble,
For alle þe golde vpon grounde I nolde go with þe,
Ne bere þe felaȝschip þurȝ þis fryth on fote fyrre."

₂₁₅₂Bi þat þe wyȝe in þe wod wendeȝ his brydel,
Hit þe hors with þe heleȝ, as harde as he myȝt,
Lepeȝ hym ouer þe launde, & leueȝ þe knyȝt þere,
al one.

₂₁₅₆"Bi Goddeȝ self," quod Gawayn,
"I wyl nauþer grete ne grone,
To Goddeȝ wylle I am ful bayn,
& to hym I haf me tone."

VIII.

₂₁₆₀Thenne gyrdeȝ he to Gryngolet, & gedereȝ þe rake,
Schowueȝ in bi a schore, at a schaȝe syde,
Rideȝ þurȝ þe roȝe bonk, ryȝt to þe dale;
& þenne he wayted hym aboute, & wylde hit hym þoȝt,

₂₁₆₄& seȝe no syngne of resette, bisydeȝ nowhere,
Bot hyȝe bonkkeȝ & brent, vpon boþe halue,
& ruȝe knokled knarreȝ, with knorned stoneȝ;
Þe skweȝ of þe scowtes skayued hym þoȝt.

₂₁₆₈Þenne he houed, & wyth-hylde his hors at þat tyde,
& ofte chaunged his cher, þe chapel to seche;

He seȝ non suche in no syde, & selly hym þoȝt,
Sone a lyttel on a launde, a lawe as hit we[re];

2172A balȝ berȝ, bi a bonke, þe brymme by-syde,
Bi a forȝ of a flode, þat ferked þare;
Þe borne blubred þer-inne, as hit boyled hade.
Þe knyȝt kacheȝ his caple, & com to þe lawe,

2176Liȝteȝ doun luflyly, & at a lynde tacheȝ
Þe rayne, & his riche, with a roȝe braunche;
Þen[n]e he boȝeȝ to þe berȝe, aboute hit he walke,
D[e]batande with hym-self, quat hit be myȝt.

2180Hit hade a hole on þe ende, & on ayþer syde,
& ouer-growen with gresse in glodes ay where,
& al watȝ holȝ in-with, nobot an olde caue,
Or a creuisse of an olde cragge, he couþe hit noȝt deme

2184with spelle,
"We, lorde," quod þe gentyle knyȝt,
"Wheþer þis be þe grene chapelle;
He myȝt aboute myd-nyȝt,

2188[Þ]e dele his matynnes telle!"

IX.

"Now i-wysse," quod Wowayn, "wysty is here;
Þis oritore is vgly, with erbeȝ ouer-growen;
Wel bisemeȝ þe wyȝe wruxled in grene

2192Dele here his deuocioun, on þe deueleȝ wyse;
Now I fele hit is þe fende, in my fyue wytteȝ,
Þat hatȝ stoken me þis steuen, to strye me here;
Þis is a chapel of meschaunce, þat chekke hit by-tyde,

₂₁₉₆Hit is þe corsedest kyrk, þat euer i com inne!"
With heȝe helme on his hede, his launce in his honde,
He romeȝ vp to þe rokke of þo roȝ woneȝ;
Þene herde he of þat hyȝe hil, in a harde roche,

₂₂₀₀Biȝonde þe broke, in a bonk, a wonder breme noyse,
Quat! hit clatered in þe clyff, as hit cleue schulde,
As one vpon a gryndelston hade grounden a syþe;
What! hit wharred, & whette, as water at a mulne,

₂₂₀₄What! hit rusched, & ronge, rawþe to here.
Þenne "bi Godde," quod Gawayn, "þat gere as I trowe,
Is ryched at þe reuerence, me renk to mete,
bi rote;

₂₂₀₈Let God worche we loo,
Hit helppeȝ me not a mote,
My lif þaȝ I for-goo,
Drede dotȝ me no lote."

X.

₂₂₁₂Thenne þe knyȝt con calle ful hyȝe,
"Who stiȝtleȝ in þis sted, me steuen to holde?
For now is gode Gawayn goande ryȝt here,
If any wyȝe oȝt wyl wynne hider fast,

₂₂₁₆Oþer now, oþer neuer, his nedeȝ to spede."
"Abyde," quod on on þe bonke, abouen ouer his hede,
"& þou schal haf al in hast, þat I þe hyȝt ones."
Ȝet he rusched on þat rurde, rapely a þrowe,

₂₂₂₀& wyth quettyng a-wharf, er he wolde lyȝt;
& syþen he keuereȝ bi a cragge, & comeȝ of a hole,
Whyrlande out of a wro, wyth a felle weppen,
A deneȝ ax nwe dyȝt, þe dynt with [t]o ȝelde

₂₂₂₄With a borelych bytte, bende by þe halme,
Fyled in a fylor, fowre fote large,
Hit watȝ no lasse, bi þat lace þat lemed ful bryȝt.
& þe gome in þe erene gered as fyrst,

₂₂₂₈Boþe þe lyre & þe leggeȝ, lokkeȝ, & berde,
Saue þat fayre on his fote he foundeȝ on þe erþe,
Sette þe stele to þe stone, & stalked bysyde.
When he wan to þe watter, þer he wade nolde,

₂₂₃₂He hypped ouer on hys ax, & orpedly strydeȝ,
Bremly broþe on a bent, þat brode watȝ a-boute,
on snawe.
Sir Gawayn þe knyȝt con mete.

₂₂₃₆He ne lutte hym no þyng lowe,
Þat oþer sayde, "now, sir swete,
Of steuen mon may þe trowe."

XI.

"Gawayn," quod þat grene gome, "God þe mot loke!

₂₂₄₀I-wysse þou art welcom, wyȝe, to my place,
& þou hatȝ tymed þi trauayl as true mon schulde;
& þou knoweȝ þe couenaunteȝ kest vus by-twene,
At þis tyme twelmonyth þou toke þat þe falled,

₂₂₄₄& I schulde at þis nwe ȝere ȝeply þe quyte.
& we ar in þis valay, verayly oure one,
Here ar no renkes vs to rydde, rele as vus likeȝ;
Haf þy helme of þy hede, & haf here þy pay;

₂₂₄₈Busk no more debate þen I þe bede þenne,
"When þou wypped of my hede at a wap one."
"Nay, bi God," quod Gawayn, "þat me gost lante,

I schal gruch þe no grwe, for grem þat falleȝ;

₂₂₅₂Botstyȝtel þe vpon on strok, & I schal stonde stylle,
& warp þe no wernyng, to worch as þe lykeȝ,
no whare."
He lened with þe nek, & lutte,

₂₂₅₆& schewed þat schyre al bare,
& lette as he noȝt dutte,
For drede he wolde not dare.

II.

Then þe gome in þe grene grayþed hym swyþe,

₂₂₆₀Gedereȝ yp hys grymme tole, Gawayn to smyte;
With alle þe bur in his body he ber hit on lofte,
Munt as maȝtyly, as marre hym he wolde;
Hade hit dryuen adoun, as dreȝ as he atled,

₂₂₆₄Þer hade ben ded of his dynt, þat doȝty watȝ euer.
Bot Gawayn on þat giserne glyfte hym bysyde,
As hit com glydande adoun, on glode hym to schende,
& schranke a lytel with þe schulderes, for þe scharp yrne.

₂₂₆₈Þat oþer schalk wyth a schunt þe schene wythhaldeȝ,
& þenne repreued he þe prynce with mony prowde wordeȝ:
"Þou art not Gawayn," quod þe gome, "þat is so goud halden,
Þat neuer arȝed for no here, by hylle ne be vale,

₂₂₇₂& now þou fles for ferde, er þou fele harmeȝ;
Such cowardise of þat knyȝt cowþe I neuer here.
Nawþer fyked I, ne flaȝe, freke, quen þou myntest,
Ne kest no kauelacion, in kyngeȝ hous Arthor,

₂₂₇₆My hede flaȝ to my fote, & ȝet flaȝ I neuer;

& þou, er any harme hent, arȝeȝ in hert,
Wherfore þe better burne me burde be called
þer-fore."

2280Quod G:, "I schunt oneȝ,
& so wyl I no more,
Bot paȝ my hede falle on þe stoneȝ,
I con not hit restore.

XIII.

2284Bot busk, burne, bi þi fayth, & bryng me to þe poynt,
Dele to me my destiné, & do hit out of honde,
For I schal stonde þe a strok, & start no more,
Til þyn ax haue me hitte, haf here my trawþe."

2288"Haf at þe þenne," quod þat oþer, & heueȝ hit alofte,
& wayteȝ as wroþely, as he wode were;
He mynteȝ at hym maȝtyly, bot not þe mon ryueȝ,
With-helde heterly h[i]s honde, er hit hurt myȝt.

2292Gawayn grayþely hit bydeȝ, & glent with no membre,
Bot stode stylle as þe ston, oþer a stubbe auþer,
Þat raþeled is in roche grounde, with roteȝ a hundreth.
Þen muryly efte con he mele, þe mon in þe grene,

2296"So now þou hatȝ þi hert holle, hitte me bihou[e]s;
Halde þe now þe hyȝe hode, þat Arþur þe raȝt,
& kepe þy kanel at þis kest, ȝif hit keuer may."
G: ful gryndelly with greme þenne sayde,

2300"Wy þresch on, þou þro mon, þou þreteȝ to longe,
I hope þat þi hert arȝe wyth þyn awen seluen."
"For soþe," quod þat oþer freke, "so felly þou spekeȝ,
I wyl no lenger on lyte lette þin ernde,

₂₃₀₄riȝt nowe."
Þenne tas he hym strype to stryke,
& frounses boþe lyppe & browe,
No meruayle þaȝ hym myslyke,

₂₃₀₈Þat hoped of no rescowe.

XIV.

He lyftes lyȝtly his lome, & let hit doun fayre,
With þe barbe of þe bitte bi þe bare nek
Þaȝ he homered heterly, hurt hym no more,

₂₃₁₂Bot snyrt hym on þat on syde, þat seuered þe hyde;
Þe scharp schrank to þe flesche þurȝ þe schyre grece,
Þat þe schene blod over his schulderes schot to þe erþe.
& quen þe burne seȝ þe blode blenk on þe snawe,

₂₃₁₆He sprit forth spenne fote more þen a spere lenþe,
Hent heterly his helme, & on his hed cast,
Schot with his schuldereȝ his fayre schelde vnder,
Braydeȝ out a bryȝt sworde, & bremely he spekeȝ;

₂₃₂₀Neuer syn þat he watȝ burne borne of his moder,
Watȝ he neuer in þis worlde, wyȝe half so blyþe:—
"Blynne, burne, of þy bur, bede me no mo;
I haf a stroke in þis sted with-oute stryf hent,

₂₃₂₄& if þow recheȝ me any mo, I redyly schal quyte,
& ȝelde ȝederly aȝayn, & þer to ȝe tryst,
& foo;
Bot on stroke here me falleȝ,

₂₃₂₈Þe couenaunt schop ryȝt so,
[Sikered] in Arþureȝ halleȝ,
& þer-fore, hende, now hoo!"

XV.

The haþel heldet hym fro, & on his ax rested,

₂₃₃₂Sette þe schaft vpon schore, & to be scharp lened,
& loked to þe leude, þat on þe launde ȝede,
How þat doȝty dredles deruely þer stondeȝ,
Armed ful aȝleȝ; in hert hit hym lykeȝ.

₂₃₃₆þenn he meleȝ muryly, wyth a much steuen,
& wyth a r[a]ykande rurde he to þe renk sayde,
"Bolde burne, on þis bent be not so gryndel;
No mon here vn-manerly þe mys-boden habbe,

₂₃₄₀Ne kyd, bot as couenaunde, at kyngeȝ kort schaped;
I hyȝt þe a strok, & þou hit hatȝ, halde þe wel payed,
I relece þe of þe remnaunt, of ryȝtes alle oþer;
ȝif I deliuer had bene, a boffet, paraunter,

₂₃₄₄I couþe wroþeloker haf waret, [&] to þe haf wroȝt anger.²
Fyrst I mansed þe muryly, with a mynt one,
& roue þe wyth no rof, sore with ryȝt I þe profered,
For þe forwarde that we fest in þe fyrst nyȝt,

₂₃₄₈& þou trystyly þe trawþe & trwly me haldeȝ,
Al þe gayne þow me gef, as god mon shulde;
Þat oþer munt for þe morne, mon, I þe profered,
Þou kyssedes my clere wyf, þe cosseȝ me raȝteȝ,

₂₃₅₂For boþe two here I þe bede bot two bare myntes,
boute scaþe;
Trwe mon trwe restore,
Þenne þar mon drede no waþe;

₂₃₅₆At þe þrid þou fayled þore,
& þer-for þat tappe ta þe.

XVI.

For hit is my wede þat þou wereȝ, þat ilke wouen girdel,
Myn owen wyf hit þe weued, I wot wel forsoþe;

₂₃₆₀Now know I wel þy cosses, & þy costes als,
& þe wowyng of my wyf, I wroȝt hit myseluen;
I sende hir to asay þe, & sothly me þynkkeȝ,
On þe fautlest freke, þat euer on fote ȝede;

₂₃₆₄As perle bi þe quite pese is of prys more,
So is Gawayn, in god fayth, bi oþer gay knyȝteȝ.
Bot here you lakked a lyttel, sir, & lewte yow wonted,
Bot þat watȝ for no wylyde werke, ne wowyng nauþer,

₂₃₆₈Bot for ȝe lufed your lyf, þe lasse I yow blame."
Þat oþer stif mon in study stod a gret whyle;
So agreued for greme he gryed with-inne,
Alle þe blode of his brest blende in his face,

₂₃₇₂Þat al he schrank for schome, þat þe schalk talked.
Þe forme worde vpon folde, þat þe freke meled,—
"Corsed worth cowarddyse & couetyse boþe!
In yow is vylany & vyse, þat vertue disstryeȝ."

₂₃₇₆Þenne he kaȝt to þe knot, & þe kest lawseȝ,
Brayde broþely þe belt to þe burne seluen:
"Lo! þer þe falssyng, foule mot hit falle!
For care of þy knokke cowardyse me taȝt

₂₃₈₀To a-corde me with couetyse, my kynde to for-sake,
Þat is larges & lewte, þat longeȝ to knyȝteȝ.
Now am I fawty, & falce, & ferde haf ben euer;
Of trecherye & vn-trawþe boþe bityde sorȝe

₂₃₈₄& care!

I bi-knowe yow, kny3t, here stylle,
Al fawty is my fare,
Lete3 me ouer-take your wylle,
& efle I schal be ware."

XVII.

Thenne lo3e þat oþer leude, & luflyly sayde,
"I halde hit hardily hole, þe harme þat I hade;
Þou art confessed so clene, be-knowen of þy mysses,

2392& hat3 þe penaunce apert, of þe poynt of myn egge,
I halde þe polysed of þat ply3t, & pured as clene,
As þou hade3 neuer forfeted, syþen þou wat3 fyrst borne.
& I gif þe, sir, þe gurdel þat is golde hemmed;

2396For hit is grene as my goune, sir G:, 3e maye
Þenk vpon þis ilke þrepe, þer þou forth þrynge3
Among prynces of prys, & þis a pure token
Of þe chaunce of þe grene chapel, at cheualrous kny3te3;

2400& 3e schal in þis nwe 3er a3ayn to my wone3,
& we schyn reuel þe remnaunt of þis ryche fest,
ful bene."
Þer laþed hym fast þe lorde,

2404& sayde, "with my wyf, I wene,
We schal yow wel acorde,
Þat wat3 your enmy kene."

XVIII.

"Nay, for soþe," quod þe segge, & sesed hys helme,

2408& hat3 hit of hendely, & þe haþel þonkke3,

"I haf soiorned sadly, sele yow bytyde,
& he ȝelde hit yow ȝare, þat ȝarkkeȝ al menskes!
& comaundeȝ me to þat cortays, your comlych fere,

2412Boþe þat on & þat oþer, myn honoured ladyeȝ.
Þat þus hor knyȝt wyth hor kest han koyntly bigyled.
Bot hit is no ferly, þaȝ a fole madde,
& þurȝ wyles of wymmen be wonen to sorȝe;

2416For so watȝ Adam in erde with one bygyled,
& Salamon with fele sere, & Samson eft soneȝ,
Dalyda dalt hym hys wyrde, & Dauyth þer-after
Watȝ blended with Barsabe, þat much bale þoled.

2420Now þese were wrathed wyth her wyles, hit were a wynne
    huge,
To luf hom wel, & leue hem not, a leude þat couþe,
For þes wer forne þe freest þat folȝed alle þe sele,
Ex-ellently of alle þyse oþer, vnder heuen-ryche,

2424þat mused;
& alle þay were bi-wyled,
With wymmen þat þay vsed,
Þaȝ I be now bigyled,

2428Me þink me burde be excused."

IX.

"Bot your gordel," quod G: "God yow for-ȝelde!
Þat wyl I welde wyth good wylle, not for þe wynne golde,
Ne þe saynt, ne þe sylk, ne þe syde pendaundes,

2432For wele, ne for worchyp, ne for þe wlonk werkkeȝ,
Bot in syngne of my surfet I schal se hit ofte;
When I ride in renoun, remorde to myseluen

Þe faut & þe fayntyse of þe flesche crabbed,

2436How tender hit is to entyse teches of fylþe;
& þus, quen pryde schal me pryk, for prowes of armes,
Þe loke to þis luf lace schal leþe my hert.
Bot on I wolde yow pray, displeses yow neuer;

2440Syn ȝe be lorde of þe ȝonde[r] londe, þer I haf lent inne,
Wyth yow wyth worschyp,—þe wyȝe hit yow ȝelde
Þat vp-haldeȝ þe heuen, & on hyȝ sitteȝ,—
How norne ȝe yowre ryȝt nome, & þenne no more?"

2444"Þat schal I telle þe trwly," quod þat oþer þenne,
"Bernlak de Hautdesert I hat in þis londe,
Þurȝ myȝt of Morgne la Faye, þat in my hous lenges,
& koyntyse of clergye, bi craftes wel lerned,

2448Þe maystres of Merlyn, mony ho taken;
For ho hatȝ dalt drwry ful dere sum tyme,
With þat conable klerk, þat knowes alle your knyȝteȝ
at hame;

2452Morgne þe goddes,
Þer-fore hit is hir name;
Weldeȝ non so hyȝe hawtesse,
Þat ho ne con make ful tame.

XX.

2456Ho wayned me vpon þis wyse to your wynne halle,
For to assay þe surquidre, ȝif hit soth were,
Þat rennes of þe grete renoun of þe Rounde Table;
Ho wayned me þis wonder, your wytteȝ to reue,

2460For to haf greued Gaynour, & gart hir to dyȝe.
With gopnyng of þat ilke gomen, þat gostlych speked,

With his hede in his honde, bifore þe hyƷe table.
Þat is ho þat is at home, þe auncian lady;

2464Ho is euen þyn aunt, ArþureƷ half suster,
Þe duches doƷter of Tyntagelle, þat dere Vter after
Hade Arþur vpon, þat aþel is nowþe.
Þerfore I eþe þe, haþel, to com to þy naunt,

2468Make myry in my hous, my meny þe louies,
& I wol þe as wel, wyƷe, bi my faythe,
As any gome vnder God, for þy grete trauþe."
& he nikked hym naye, he nolde bi no wayes;

2472Þay acolen & kyssen, [bikennen] ayþer oþer
To þe prynce of paradise, & parten ryƷt þere,
on coolde;
Gawayn on blonk ful bene,

2476To þe kyngeƷ burƷ buskeƷ bolde,
& þe knyƷt in þe enker grene,
Whider-warde so euer he wolde.

XXI.

Wylde wayeƷ in þe worlde Wowen now rydeƷ,

2480On Gryngolet, þat þe grace hade geten of his lyue;
Ofte he herbered in house, & ofte al þeroute,
& mony a-venture in vale, & venquyst ofte,
Þat I ne tyƷt, at þis tyme, in tale to remene.

2484Þe hurt watƷ hole, þat he hade hent in his nek,
& þe blykkande belt he bere þeraboute,
A belef as a bauderyk, bounden bi his syde,
Loken vnder his lyfte arme, þe lace, with a knot,

$_{2488}$In tokenyng he watȝ tane in tech of a faute;
& þus he commes to þe court, knyȝt al in sounde.
Þer wakned wele in þat wone, when wyst þe grete,
Þat gode G: watȝ commen, gayn hit hym þoȝt;

$_{2492}$Þe kyng kysseȝ þe knyȝt, & þe whene alce,
& syþen mony syker knyȝt, þat soȝt hym to haylce,
Of his fare þat hym frayned, & ferlyly he telles;
Biknowoȝ alle þe costes of care þat he hade,——

$_{2496}$Þe chaunce of þe chapel, þe chere of þe knyȝt,
Þe luf of þe ladi, þe lace at þe last.
Þe nirt in þe nek he naked hem schewed,
Þat he laȝt for his vnleute at þe leudes hondes,

$_{2500}$for blame;
He tened quen he schulde telle,
He groned for gref & grame;
Þe blod in his face con melle,

$_{2504}$When he hit schulde schewe, for schame.

XXII.

"Lo! lorde," quod þe leude, & þe lace hondeled,
"Þis is þe bende of þis blame I bere [in] my nek,
Þis is þe laþe & þe losse, þat I laȝt haue,

$_{2508}$Of couardise & couetyse, þat I haf caȝt þare,
Þis is þe token of vn-trawþe, þat I am tan inne,
& I mot nedeȝ hit were, wyle I may last;
For non may hyden his harme, bot vnhap ne may hit,

$_{2512}$For þer hit oneȝ is tachched, twynne wil hit neuer."
Þe kyng comforteȝ þe knyȝt, & alle þe court als,
Laȝen loude þer-at, & luflyly acorden,

Þat lordes & ladis, þat longed to þe Table,

2516Vche burne of þe broþer-hede a bauderyk schulde haue,
A bende, a belef hym aboute, of a bry3t grene,
& þat, for sake of þat segge, in swete to were.
For þat wat3 acorded þe renoun of þe Rounde Table,

2520& he honoured þat hit hade, euer-more after,
As hit is breued in þe best boke of romaunce.
Þus in Arthurus day þis aunter bitidde,
Þe Brutus bokees þer-of beres wyttenesse;

2524Syþen Brutus, þe bolde burne, bo3ed hider fyrst,
After þe segge & þe asaute wat3 sesed at Troye,
I-wysse;
Mony auntere3 here bi-forne,

2528Haf fallen suche er þis:
Now þat bere þe croun of þorne,
He bryng vus to his blysse! AMEN.

Made in the USA
Coppell, TX
19 January 2022

71945469R00069